MORMONISM: IMPOSSIBLE

MORMONISM: IMPOSSIBLE

Refuting a Fundamental Mormon Doctrine and

Using Apologetics to Reach the Latter-Day Saints

NACE HOWELL

XULON PRESS

Xulon Press
555 Winderley Pl, Suite 225
Maitland, FL 32751
407.339.4217
www.xulonpress.com

Unless otherwise noted, all Scripture is taken from The Holy Bible: King
James Version., electronic ed. of the 1769 edition of the 1611 Authorized
Version.

Paperback ISBN-13: 9781662885372
Hard Cover ISBN-13: 9781662885389
eBook ISBN-13: 9781662885396

To my amazing wife, Bethany. My true love, my best friend, my confidante. Thank you for being my mentor in life, love, compassion, patience, gentleness, forgiveness, and grace.

Contents

Introduction ix

Chapter 1 ~ The Pillar and Ground of Truth. 1

Chapter 2 ~ Exposition and Defense of the Doctrine
of Exaltation 11

Chapter 3 ~ Heavenly Father, His Dwelling Place,
and His Prophet. 43

Chapter 4 ~ Biblical and Philosophical Arguments Against
the Doctrine of Exaltation. 92

Chapter 5 ~ The Devastating Archaeological Assertions 118

Chapter 6 ~ A Biblical and Logical Defense of
Christianity Against Mormonism 130

Chapter 7 ~ Apologetics and Evangelism to Mormons 150

Appendix ~ Memorable Questions to Ask Mormons 181

Sources Cited 183

Index 191

Introduction

MORMONS (THAT IS, members of the Church of Jesus Christ of the Latter-day Saints)[1] claim some very specific details about the reality of God and about the reality of human beings. Imagine that you are traveling in a commercial airplane that is unlike any other. From its windows, you can magically see events as if they are moving through time at an extremely fast pace. As you look down at the earth, you see people being born, living, and dying, but you also see people *after* they die. Mormonism teaches what is called the doctrine of exaltation which is mostly found in what they consider to be one of their four primary texts of Holy Scriptures titled *Doctrine and Covenants*, as well as in other places within the official beliefs of the Latter-day Saint religion.

The doctrine of exaltation is the fundamental teaching in The Church of Jesus Christ of the Latter-day Saints which maintains that any man can become a god when he dies, *if* he has lived a good enough life, and specifically did not murder anyone.[2] The doctrine of exaltation also teaches that the Mormon god is an exalted human man

---

[1] I realize that the Mormon president recently suggested that they should not be referred to as *Mormons* any longer, but this did not register because people apparently do not like typing out "Church of Jesus Christ of the Latter-Day Saints," and also because I, and others like me, prefer not to attach the name of Jesus to Mormonism, so I will continue to refer to such using the terms *Mormon(s)* and *Mormonism*.

[2] Joseph Smith. *The Doctrine and Covenants of the Church of Jesus Christ of the Latter-day Saints* (Salt Lake City: The Church of Jesus Christ of the Latter-day Saints; Intellectual Reserve), 1981. Section 132:19–20 and 42:18; More on this in Chapter Two.

from another planet.[3] The doctrine of exaltation teaches that the way a man becomes a god is by following a specific set of rules that have been translated, recorded, and prophesied by their prophet, Joseph Smith, from the Mormon god in the *Book of Mormon*, the *Doctrine and Covenants*, the *Pearl of Great Price*, and various sermons and writings from Joseph Smith as well as several presidents and "apostles" within the Mormon Church.[4]

The doctrine of exaltation (or any of the primary sacred Mormon scriptures) does not teach *why* men become gods, or how it is even possible, which answering the question, "why?" is the major focus of this book. The ultimate question I am asking is, "Why is it the case that men can become gods?" as well as what the implications are that the answers to this question provide, which are found in their scriptures.

From fifty thousand feet above ground, *why* are men becoming gods? When we look down on the world from the hypothetical airplane and see people after they die becoming gods over and over, it raises the question, even from the Mormon perspective, "Why is it happening?" Mormons are making a truth claim about reality through their scriptures that men become gods, and by doing so, they are claiming that this is ultimate reality ... that it is *possible* that men[5] can become gods.

---

[3] Gerald N. Lund, *Is President Lorenzo Snow's oft-repeated statement—"As man now is, God once was; as God now is, man may be"—accepted as official doctrine by the Church?* (1982): https://abn.churchofjesuschrist.org/study/ensign/1982/02/i-have-a-question/is-president-snows-statement-as-man-now-is-god-once-was-as-god-now-is-man-may-be-accepted-as-official-doctrine.html?lang=eng; See also, *Doctrine and Covenants* 93:29-35; Joseph Smith. *Pearl of Great Price*. (Salt Lake City: The Church of Jesus Christ of the Latter-day Saints; Intellectual Reserve), 1981. Abraham 3:18–28.

[4] Joseph Smith. *The Book of Mormon: Another Testament of Jesus Christ* (Salt Lake City: The Church of Jesus Christ of the Latter-day Saints; Intellectual Reserve), 1981. See also, above citations.

[5] I have been corrected by Mormons on using the word "men" because they did not want me to think that it was only for men. From their belief, it is also the case that women can become gods, which will be elaborated on in chapter two. This correction is purely a Red Herring, seeking to distract from the actual argument.

Not only is it possible, according to Mormonism, it has been happening for an infinite regress of time (that is, time going backwards for an infinite amount, but not forward because we stop at the event of *today*).[6]

Along with the question of why this is happening, another question arises, which is, "Is the doctrine of exaltation true?" I hope to unveil some truths about the reality of God in the following pages concerning both of these questions. The reason they need to be asked is because Mormons themselves do not seem to ask, yet these are fundamental and reasonable questions. In my numerous conversations with Mormons, I find that they do not ask one another, and they generally do not metaphysically process such. This is perhaps because they have not thought through these questions or thought beyond their own scriptures (or they are afraid to ask these questions because of what truths may result), so it could be difficult to navigate a conversation in dealing with such things.

My hope is that this book will help equip the reader to navigate such a conversation and cultivate seeds of doubt within the Mormon mind; to help him or her think through the problems that the Mormon doctrine of exaltation presents, and by nature of relation, the problems that Mormonism itself presents. I also seek to present answers to these questions for any inquiring member of the Church of Jesus Christ of the Latter-day Saints and to help him understand what his scriptures say (or do not say) about such things.

---

[6] In fact, we will discover throughout this volume how infinite regress is a requirement for the logical consistency of the doctrine of exaltation.

Chapter One:

The Pillar and Ground of Truth

"But if I tarry long, that thou mayest know how thou oughtest to behave thyself in **the house of God, which is the church of the living God, the pillar and ground of the truth**." ~ 1 Timothy 3:15

AS NOTED IN the introduction, the ultimate question this book seeks to answer is from the Mormon perspective, "Why is it the case that men become gods?" The question itself raises the question, "Is the doctrine of exaltation true?" Another reason for evaluating the doctrine of exaltation is because Mormons claim that this is the ultimate reality about God ... the truth about God. In other words, according to Mormonism, historical, biblical Christianity[7] has been incorrect about the reality of God for millennia, and Mormonism (or, more specifically, Joseph Smith), has come along to correct this wrong thinking.

The material for this book came about through a lifelong curiosity concerning Mormonism, from having encounters with Mormons all my adult life, sparking an interest for further research about what they teach, and what powerfully developed into a deep desire to pursue the truth claims in Mormonism about reality, specifically the reality about God.

In some of my conversations with people, I ask them privately, or perhaps in a counseling setting what they believe is wrong with the

---

[7] A Christian is simply a follower of Jesus Christ as described in the Bible (See Acts 11:26).

world. The surprising part is that I find this to be one of the most thorough and efficient ways to quickly discover the things that someone is truly passionate about. Instead of asking what they like to do or what their hobbies are, in order to discover their spiritual gifts and personal passions, it seems better to start with the idea of what they think is wrong with the world. Often, such answers regard sexual or other types of abuse, or on a more positive note, it has something to do with the teaching of children. For my own case, I would answer this question of what is wrong with the world with one word, *lies*. To elaborate, it is falsehood and inaccuracy concerning reality, theology, and apologetics (i.e. a rational defense for the Christian faith) that deeply concerns me. I am passionate about discovering what the truth is, and guiding people to the truth (i.e. that which corresponds to reality).

Also, I have come through the years to think of myself as a protector of persons, much like a shepherd. I am passionate about protecting the truth (reality) about the church (the body of Christ), the truth concerning Christianity, and obviously the truth of the gospel. The Bible says that the church is to be the "pillar and ground of the truth."[8] With these things in mind, along with the fact that I am surrounded by Mormons in the Indian reservation where I live, being passionate about the truth and having a deep desire to protect and defend the truth, one can get a good idea of how this all got started.

What Is the Objective?

The primary aim of this book is that it is used by God through families, co-workers, and friends of Mormons to bring them into a knowledge of the truth about Him so that they might come to a place of repentance and know the true God and Jesus Christ whom God has sent.[9] Mormonism, I will argue, is a result of the work of the devil, leading

---

[8] The King James Version is the accepted version of the Bible according to Mormons, and so this will be the primary translation cited in this book, 1 Ti. 3:15.

[9] See Jn 17:3.

people astray from the true word of God and away from a real and saving relationship with Jesus. Because it is a work of the devil, I want to bring these fundamental Mormon beliefs out into the open so that they can simply be examined without secrecy, mystery, and deception.

There are other purposes as well. One simply being that readers learn more about Mormonism. Apologetics, specifically counter-cult apologetics, calls for more than just knowledge of the Bible; it also calls for people to not be in the dark when it comes to other faiths. Through the content in this book, people who have Mormon friends, neighbors, and relatives will have some knowledge of fundamental and essential Mormon doctrine and will be able to articulate the truth concerning the logic of such a doctrine both philosophically and theologically.

Another purpose is to directly help those who are seeking truth,[10] discover the truth about Mormonism (and Christianity, indirectly). Everyone needs to find the truth of the one true God and Lord Jesus,[11] and if Mormonism were not even available as a religious option, perhaps one who is seeking truth, peace, and hope might not be deceived into consuming *la dolce vita* falsely offered in Mormonism and bypass it altogether. It looks very appetizing to some, with its fine, wholesome ingredients such as eggs, flour, milk, and sugar, but it also has lethal poison in the recipe, finished with thick, creamy icing and biblical truths sprinkled all over the top. To the untrained eye, it can look extremely appetizing. If the poison is understood when someone is reading the recipe, then they will want nothing to do with it, and the recipe will be discarded and forgotten.

I find that in my own quest for discovering the truth about such things, Mormonism is deeply flawed at its core; at its foundation (the doctrine of exaltation, specifically), and there are so many people in the world, especially in the United States of America, who unquestioningly believe this doctrine to be true. The real problem, I believe, is that

---

[10] See Mt. 7:7–8.

[11] See Ro. 3:23.

Mormonism does not accurately describe the truth about the reality of God. My heart is to see these misleading Mormon doctrines exposed for what they are, and I desire that Christians become more equipped to show how and why Mormonism is false and why Christianity is true.

The doctrine of exaltation (which again, is basically the idea that human beings, men in particular, can potentially become gods), is fundamental and foundational to Mormonism, and if the foundation of the structure of Mormonism is weak and crumbling, then the whole structure will collapse. Much like a faulty and fractured bridge abutment will eventually collapse the entire bridge. This destruction is the ultimate goal, which amounts to Mormons repenting of their sins and coming to know "the only true God, and Jesus Christ whom He has sent."[12] It seems that one way to help a Mormon understand that his belief system fails miserably at its foundation, both philosophically and theologically speaking, would be to show that the things required for the doctrine of exaltation to be true are actually false. This will be covered throughout this book.

Another major reason I wanted to research this is because in my numerous conversations with Mormons, both in person and online, I find that when they are confronted with the idea that they believe that they may one day become gods, they often make it sound as if the doctrine of exaltation is crazy talk at first, so this is why I wanted to make sure that I knew what I was talking about when it came to the actual beliefs that Mormons hold concerning the doctrine of exaltation, and what their sacred scriptures teach about such. I find in my conversations with Mormons that they thoroughly and completely believe that they will one day become gods. Because there are a few Mormons who seem to deny the doctrine of exaltation found within their own scriptures and official teachings, perhaps a relevant question might be, "What is the reason to deny the doctrine of exaltation if their scriptures teach it and the adherents of Mormonism believe it?" It

---

[12] See Jn. 17:3; Author's translation.

seems to me that one of the two main reasons for this denial might be the equivalent to the doctrine of Taqiyya in Islam, which is essentially a denial of specific religious beliefs in order to make Islam seem more palatable.[13] Perhaps another reason to deny the doctrine of exaltation is that the Mormon with whom one is having a discussion with simply has not yet reached this understanding of the doctrines found in his own religion.

Getting Down to Brass Tacks: Part One

Some discoveries I have made in my conversations with Mormons are shocking from a historical (or even an evangelical) Christian perspective. I also find that in my countless discussions with Mormons they always seem to believe what is commonly known and described about them in the world of apologetics.

In the beginning of my discussions and conversations with Mormons, I mostly have one agenda, which is to get the truth about what the person in front of me really believes. Is everything I read about Mormonism from a Christian apologetics perspective perfectly accurate to his actual beliefs? I want to always be gentle in my approach to receive honest and unbiased testimonies. I am always curious to know if the members of the Mormon Church I am speaking with view themselves as postmodern, religiously speaking. What I mean by that is I want to see if my Mormon friend generally thinks it is okay to dabble in other religions and take what he likes from them, as if religions of the world were offered buffet style. I do not frequently find this thought process in my interactions with Mormons, although I have indeed encountered a few. The issue of postmodernity comes up in my mind because of what Mormons call *the Moroni Challenge*, which is a challenge from Mormons to non-Mormons

---

[13] See Sura 3:28 in the Quran for the source of *Taqiyya*. This is where Muslims can deny their religious beliefs or practices in order to make new converts. There are several similarities between Islam and Mormonism, and more of these will be discussed in chapter three.

to *feel* that the Book of Mormon is true from the Book of Mormon itself, found in Moroni chapter 10 verses 3-5 and 27-29. The second paragraph is the heart of the Moroni challenge:

> Behold, I would exhort you that when ye shall read these things, if it be wisdom in God that ye should read them, that ye would remember how merciful the Lord hath been unto the children of men, from the creation of Adam even down until the time that ye shall receive these things, and ponder it in your hearts.
>
> And when ye shall receive these things, I would exhort you that ye would ask God, the Eternal Father, in the name of Christ, if these things are not true; and if ye shall ask with a sincere heart, with real intent, having faith in Christ, he will manifest the truth of it unto you, by the power of the Holy Ghost.
>
> And by the power of the Holy Ghost ye may know the truth of all things....
>
> And I exhort you to remember these things; for the time speedily cometh that ye shall know that I lie not, for ye shall see me at the bar of God; and the Lord God will say unto you: Did I not declare my words unto you, which were written by this man, like as one crying from the dead, yea, even as one speaking out of the dust?
>
> I declare these things unto the fulfilling of the prophecies. And behold, they shall proceed forth out of the mouth of the everlasting God; and his word shall hiss forth from generation to generation.
>
> And God shall show unto you, that that which I have written is true.[14]

---

[14] *The Book of Mormon*, 10:3–5; 27–29.

Postmodernism will be examined later, but for now, one can see that from the Moroni challenge, there are obvious hints of postmodernism and the idea that the heart is the instrument used to discern what is true or false in Mormonism.

I am also curious to know how Mormons truly feel about becoming like *Heavenly Father* (a title that is interchangeable with the word *"god"* within Mormonism), as in, if they *really and truly* believe that it is possible to have the same status as Heavenly Father. Often, Mormons will evade the question when asked, but I desire to get to the bottom of it when discussing such things with an individual. We should have gentleness and respect, but it is still appropriate to seek the truth of what is believed. I will also ask this question in different ways because I want to make sure that the question I am really seeking is understood. I find that it is common among Christian apologists to question the reality about God concerning such Mormon beliefs. This seems to show that there is a common understanding regarding the doctrines on such.

I also like to discover how much a Mormon actually knows about his or her own faith. No matter what kind of religion one adheres to, there is always room for learning more about such. In Mormonism, the case is not different. There are Mormons who claim to be Mormon yet have no real idea about what many of the doctrines teach in Mormonism, simply because they have not been exposed to them yet or perhaps that they have not yet thought through them. To be able to discover how much a Mormon knows about his faith, one should have a good grasp on Mormonism, which a person can arguably obtain from reading Christian apologetics literature on the topic.

Some Mormons will tell me that the doctrine of exaltation is not important, but instead, what is important is *how* one should live. But since the doctrine of exaltation is foundational and fundamental to the Latter-day Saints, it only makes sense that they really believe that the doctrine of exaltation is important indeed.

The Lorenzo Snow Couplet is one of the major things that kept running through my head in order to provoke the subject material for this book. The couplet reads as follows: "As man now is, God once was; as God now is, man may become."[15] I have encountered the couplet so many times in my apologetics research that I quickly committed it to memory, and while out doing everyday life, such as four-wheeling, fly-fishing, changing the oil in my motorcycle, or other simple activities, I often find myself reflecting on the couplet. Because of this, I have frequently argued with it in my mind from both biblical and philosophical perspectives. I have heard in several personal interviews with Mormons that the couplet does not matter much because Lorenzo Snow said it before he was officially the President of the Church. There are several issues with this claim as well, such as, when did the President receive his authority, and from where did he receive it? What if the Church of Jesus Christ of the Latter-day Saints says that the couplet is official doctrine? This would not be an issue, but many Mormons that I speak with believe that the president of the Latter-day Saints church received his authority as a prophet of God before he became president, and that he received this authority from God. Thus, the claim that the Lorenzo Snow Couplet is invalid, *is itself invalid* in Mormon theology (We will explore this more later).

I also like to ask questions in my conversations on how Mormons view the nature of their god through the perspective of time. In other words, I want to get to the bottom of the idea that Mormons worship an exalted man. As in, *how human is the Mormon God right now*? The process of Exaltation (man becoming a god) could not go on forever for multiple reasons, which will be examined in chapter four.

Many Mormons, I find, believe that their god is a human alien from another planet who has reached (*or is eternally reaching*) the end goal of godhood. This follows logically from what the Mormon scriptures teach, but what is inconsistent is the belief of such from one Mormon to the next. In other words, not all Mormons believe that their god began

---

[15] Gerald N. Lund, *Is President Lorenzo Snow's oft-repeated statement—"As man now is, God once was; as God now is, man may be"—accepted as official doctrine by the Church?* (1982); emphasis added.

as a human alien from another planet in this universe. This is why it is important to discover the personal beliefs of the person with whom one is speaking. It appears that these inconsistencies across the board in such beliefs stem from a wide array of beliefs about the doctrine of exaltation, which is to be expected.

Summary

Living in an open Indian reservation in the Rocky Mountains, as a Christian I am surrounded by not only Buddhists, Jehovah's Witnesses, Baha'i, New Agers, atheists, and traditional religions, but also, to a high degree, Mormons. I am genuinely curious to hear everyone's story. In my conversations with Mormons, I find that they often try to distract from the questions of the doctrine of exaltation or play it off as something perhaps arbitrary. It is because of such that I am always curious to see what their real beliefs are concerning the doctrine of exaltation, and what local individual Mormons actually believe about all the books and articles I have been reading about Mormonism. I find their beliefs are accurate to what I have learned throughout my adult life. It turns out that what I have read about Mormonism is accurate, particularly that the doctrine of exaltation is a strongly held belief that is common among Mormons, and I want to reveal this to anyone reading this book. In general, I also want to help equip a person to combat the false teaching of the doctrine of exaltation and Mormonism.

The reality about God comes into question because there are so many religious options out there. If one were sheltered all his life and dumped into a library full of religious artifacts (much like what is in this Indian reservation with its many very diverse religions), what would be the outcome? The Holy Spirit has access to our inner being, and because of such, either we invite the truth about Jesus into our being and make Him our Lord and Savior, or we suppress such truth. We can be so close, yet still be so far away from the truth. This is the case with Mormons. Therefore as a Christian, one should "Sanctify the Lord God in your hearts: and be ready always to give an *answer* to every man that asketh you a reason of the hope that is in you with meekness and fear."[16] Not only this, but we should also *contend for the faith* as Jude charges his readers to do.[17] The reason we need to *contend for the faith* is not because Christianity needs to be fought for, because the truth will take care of itself, in a sense. But the problem is that people need help understanding. People need help to think straight. Once they can think straight on their own (true Christian thinking is straight thinking), then they should disciple others as well and obey the Great Commission.

> *"Go ye therefore, and teach all nations, baptizing them in the name of the Father, and of the Son, and of the Holy Ghost: Teaching them to observe all things whatsoever I have commanded you: and, lo, I am with you always, even unto the end of the world. Amen."*
> ~ Matthew 28:19–20

---

[16] 1 Pt. 3:15; emphasis added.

[17] Jude 3; emphasis added.

Chapter Two:

Exposition and Defense of the Doctrine of Exaltation

"God himself was once as we are now, and is an exalted man, and sits enthroned in yonder heavens! That is the great secret." ~ Joseph Smith

THERE IS AT this point a need for a clear understanding of who is the Mormon god. Since it is most likely that the readers of this book are Christian and not Mormon, not only will the following distinction and comparison help the Christian reader further understand the difference between the two deities, but it will also further help the Christian reader understand who the Mormon god is, and how Mormons view their *Heavenly Father* (as we will, from now on, distinguish the Mormon god from the Christian God in this book). Moreover, it is also the hope that the further exposure of the doctrine of exaltation in this chapter is agreed upon as accurate by Mormons themselves, and their understanding of their scripture.

The Christian God Compared to the Mormon Heavenly Father

The Christian God is biblically and theologically speaking, Trinitarian. That is, there are three persons in one being. In the Bible, which is one of the four sacred texts of the Mormons, we should perhaps first look at the *Shema*, which is found in Deuteronomy chapter six, verse four. It reads: "Hear, O Israel: The Lord our God is one Lord."[18]

From this, it is clear that God is one being. Next, we should perhaps examine John chapter one, verses one through three, which says, "In the beginning was the Word, and the Word was with God, and the Word was God. The same was in the beginning with God. All things were made by him; and without him was not any thing made that was made."[19] Jesus (the Word) was there before the beginning, and through Him all things were made. So, God is one being and exists in the Father and the Son at this point in our discussion, biblically speaking. We will discuss the person of the Holy Spirit, biblically speaking, in chapter four. The point I want to make here is that Mormons do not believe in the Trinitarian God, but they instead believe in what is known as tritheism, which is essentially three gods. There are several other passages in the Bible which speak to the Trinitarian doctrine as well,[20] which we will discuss many of these in much greater detail in chapter four, but for now, such will suffice for our purposes here.

Not only is God Trinitarian in nature according to His own Word, but John also records Jesus saying that "God is spirit, and those who worship him must worship in spirit and truth."[21] This a very different picture than what Mormons believe about the reality of God.

On the contrary to the Christian God, the Mormon god is an *exalted man*. In *Doctrine and Covenants* section one hundred and thirty, verse twenty-two, Joseph Smith writes, "The Father has a body of flesh and bones as tangible as man's; the Son also; but the Holy Ghost has not a body of flesh and bones, but is a personage of Spirit. Were it not so,

---

[18] Dt. 6:4.

[19] Jn. 1:1–3.

[20] See also Jn. 10:30; chapter 17; Mk. chapter 1; Mt. 28:19–20; Several Christophanies in the Old Testament, Ex. 31:3; Ps. 51; Re. 1:8; 17, 18; et al.

[21] Jn. 4:24.

the Holy Ghost could not dwell in us."[22] The reason that "the Father" has a body of flesh and bones as tangible as a man's body is because "the Father" *was* a man, and clearly still is in some respect. We can also see this same idea elaborated on from the *Scriptural Teachings … of Joseph Smith* on the Mormon scriptures:

> *I will go back to the beginning before the world was, to show what kind of being God is. What sort of a being was God in the beginning? Open your ears and hear, all ye ends of the earth, for I am going to prove it to you by the Bible, and to tell you the designs of God in relation to the human race, and why He interferes with the affairs of man.*
>
> *God himself was once as we are now, and is an exalted man, and sits enthroned in yonder heavens! That is the great secret. If the veil were rent today, and the great God who holds this world in its orbit, and who upholds all worlds and all things by his power, was to make himself visible,—I say, if you were to see him today, you would see him like a man in form—like yourselves in all the person, image, and very form as a man; for Adam was created in the very fashion, image and likeness of God, and received instruction from, and walked, talked and conversed with him, as one man talks and communes with another.*[23]

So, Heavenly Father is not only an exalted man (i.e. the same species as man with flesh and bones), he is also not a Trinitarian God. He could not possibly be Trinitarian in nature simply based on the fact

---

[22] *Doctrine and Covenants*, 130:22.

[23] Joseph Smith. *Scriptural Teachings of the Prophet Joseph Smith*. (Salt Lake City: Deseret Book Company, 1938), 345. https://scriptures.byu.edu/stpjs.html. Italics in original.

that he was once a man. Not only that, but Heavenly Father could not possibly be the Greatest Conceivable Being because of the fact that he was once a man. On top of all of this, according to the doctrine of exaltation, because Heavenly Father was once a man, he absolutely had a *beginning*. In other words, the God of Mormonism is a created being. So, which is it that best describes the reality about God? Is God eternal or is he finite? Was God born as a man or has he been the same God from eternity past, present, and future? The truth about God cannot be both of these, since they absolutely contradict one another. These and many other issues and inconsistencies come up about the reality of God between Mormonism and Christianity, especially considering that Mormons claim to be Christians.[24]

How Does One Become a God in the Mormon Religion?

Probably the best place to begin this discussion is from the sacred Mormon scripture, *Doctrine and Covenants*, section one hundred and thirty-two. In order to avoid being accused of not using the full context, we will look at verses nineteen through twenty-three.

> And again, verily I say unto you, *if a man marry a wife by my word, which is my law*, and by the new and everlasting covenant, and it is sealed unto them by the Holy Spirit of promise, by him who is anointed, unto whom I have appointed this power and the keys of this priesthood; and it shall be said unto them—Ye shall come forth in the first resurrection; and if it be after the first resurrection, in the next resurrection; and shall inherit thrones, kingdoms, principalities, and powers, dominions, all heights and depths—then shall it be

---

[24] Mormons will frequently say when asked if they are Christian, that it is obvious that they are because the name of Jesus Christ is in the name of their church, but this has several issues, which will be discussed throughout this book.

written in the Lamb's Book of Life, that *he shall commit no murder whereby to shed innocent blood, and if ye abide in my covenant,* and commit no murder whereby to shed innocent blood, it shall be done unto them in all things whatsoever my servant hath put upon them, in time, and through all eternity; and shall be of full force when they are out of the world; and *they shall pass by the angels, and the gods, which are set there, to their Exaltation* and glory in all things, as hath been sealed upon their heads, which glory shall be a fullness and a continuation of the seeds forever and ever.

Then shall they be gods, because they have no end; therefore shall they be from everlasting to everlasting, because they continue; then shall they be above all, because all things are subject unto them. *Then shall they be gods,* because they have call power, and the angels are subject unto them.

Verily, verily, I say unto you, except ye abide my law ye cannot attain to this glory. For strait is the gate, and narrow the way that leadeth unto the *Exaltation* and continuation of the lives, and few there be that find it, because ye receive me not in the world neither do ye know me.

But if ye receive me in the world, then shall ye know me, and shall receive your *Exaltation*; that where I am ye shall be also.[25]

So then, in this context, one can understand that in order for a person to achieve godhood, also known as Exaltation, a man must "marry a wife by *my word, which is my law*" and "shall commit no

---

[25] *Doctrine and Covenants*, 132:19–23; emphasis added.

murder…" and "abide in my covenant." This passage and others make the doctrine of exaltation undeniably extant in Mormon scriptures.[26]

If one were curious what Joseph Smith is referring to as "law" in the citation above, he can see the definition at work also from an earlier verse in section one hundred and thirty-two of the *Doctrine and Covenants*: "I am the Lord thy God; and I give unto you this commandment—that no man shall come unto the Father but by me or by *my word, which is my law*, saith the Lord."[27] This verse, with the beginning of verse nineteen in the above citation, makes it clear to what is being referred. This seems to bring a conflict of interest into play…. The *"law"* then, is *"the word of the Lord"* which could really be anything that Joseph Smith determines is spoken by the Lord, since he is supposedly the "Prophet" who records everything that the Lord says:

> Joseph Smith, *the Prophet and Seer of the Lord*, has done more, save Jesus only, for the salvation of men in this world, than any other man that ever lived in it. In the short space of twenty years, he has brought forth the *Book of Mormon*, which he translated by the gift and power of God, and has been the means of publishing it on two continents; has sent the fullness of the everlasting gospel, which it contained, to the four quarters of the earth; has brought forth the revelations and commandments which compose this book of *Doctrine and Covenants*, and many other

---

[26] See *Doctrine and Covenants* 14:7; 76:59–70; 84:20–2; 131:1–4; 132:16–17; 37; *Alma*, In the *Book of Mormon*, 34:32–34 (The official website attributes what is said here in Alma to the doctrine of exaltation. See Church of Jesus Christ of the Latter-day Saints. *Gospel Principles*, Intellectual Reserve, Incorporated, 2011). Chapter 47. https://www.churchofjesuschrist.org/study/manual/gospel-principles/chapter-47-Exaltation?lang=eng); the *Scriptural Teachings of the Prophet Joseph Smith* citation above; et al.

[27] *Doctrine and Covenants*, 132:12; emphasis added.

wise documents and instructions for the benefit of the children of men....[28]

Another interesting thing to point out here is that the event of Exaltation is described in section one hundred and thirty-two above, as "glory" in verse twenty-one. So, Exaltation is achieving the *ultimate glory*. It is essentially, *the glory of the gods*.

It seems at this point since I mentioned *gods* (plural), there should be some clarity on what specifically Mormons should be classified as, considering their worldview (the way a person views the world). Many Christians have historically classified Mormons as polytheists (i.e. the belief in and worship of many gods), but because they only worship one god, and yet acknowledge many, simply because the doctrine of exaltation explicitly implies the existence of innumerable gods, Mormons are, I will argue, better classified as *henotheists* (i.e. the belief that many gods exist but with the direct worship of only one), if they indeed believe what their own scriptures teach, which the reader will continue to find that a majority of them do believe their own scriptures.

In the book, *See the Gods Fall*, by Francis Beckwith and Stephen Parrish, the authors describe Mormons as being either polytheistic or monarchotheistic (i.e. the belief that one Supreme God exists over a set of all other gods, i.e., Mormon gods).[29] Perhaps there are some who hold to monarchotheism in more intellectual circles who recognize the need for a law to be put into effect for the pattern of human Mormons becoming gods to exist, but I find that Mormons typically believe in their Heavenly Father as the only object of their worship, and also being the "one supreme god," while not denying other gods of equal existence. This is henotheism. Henotheism, remember, is the belief that many gods may exist, but the focus of worship is only directed

---

[28] *Doctrine and Covenants*, 135:3; emphasis added.

[29] Francis Beckwith and Stephen Parrish, *See the Gods Fall: Four rivals to Christianity* (Joplin: College Press Publishing Company, 1997), 97.

toward one specific deity, such as Heavenly Father. Mormon scriptures do not directly teach monarchotheism or henotheism. Henotheism is more of an accurate description than polytheism, and I find that most practicing Mormons come to appreciate the label of henotheism once it is understood. One issue here is that Mormons do not worship their Heavenly Father *and* the monarchical god that is above all those who have become gods in Mormonism, but *only* Heavenly Father. Mormons seem to be more inclined to label themselves as henotheists rather than monarchotheists. This is likely because they do not want to admit a god exists who is superior to or supreme over Heavenly Father.

Monarchotheism acknowledges a superior being over and above the Mormon object of worship, which is what differentiates it from henotheism. Both recognize that there is more than one god, but monarchotheism sees a god existing above a set of gods, where henotheism maintains that there is a set of gods where all deities are equal in the sense of godhood.

Since there is no mention whatsoever in Mormon scripture that describes a supreme being over the collection of Heavenly Fathers, and the issue of admitting such as discussed above, Mormons adopting the term monarchotheism for themselves would prove to be very difficult, based on their own usage and their scriptures' usage of the phrase, *Supreme Being*, which will be discussed at length in chapter three. Of the hundreds of conversations that I have had regarding such things with Mormons, not one of them were monarchotheistic, and were often completely puzzled at the thought of monarchotheism. I believe this confusion comes from logical compartmentalization. The objective here is that Mormons need to understand the implications of the doctrine of exaltation, not compartmentalized, but integrated with the rest of their theology and logic, so they can see what Mormon doctrine ultimately logically requires. Once the integration of these thoughts take place, the Mormon must come to grips with (or struggle through) the logical and biblical inconsistencies therein, which will be discussed throughout this book.

There are several other places in Latter-day Saint sacred writing that mention and often blatantly teach the doctrine of exaltation. As previously mentioned, there is a famous couplet spoken by the Fifth Mormon President, Lorenzo Snow, which we find in context in the following citation from the Church of Jesus Christ of Latter-day Saints *official* website:

> According to Elder Snow, "While attentively listening to his explanation, the Spirit of the Lord rested mightily upon me—the eyes of my understanding were opened, and I saw as clear as the sun at noonday, with wonder and astonishment, the pathway of God and man. I formed the following couplet which expresses the revelation, as it was shown me, and explains Father Smith's dark saying to me at a blessing meeting in the Kirtland Temple, prior to my baptism...
> "As man now is, God once was:"
> "As God now is, man may be."
> "I *felt* this to be a sacred communication, which I related to no one except my sister Eliza, until I reached England, when in a confidential private conversation with President Brigham Young, in Manchester, I related to him this extraordinary manifestation." (Eliza R. Snow, pp. 46–47; Brigham Young was President of the Quorum of the Twelve at the time).[30]

This couplet, which I find that many Mormons have never heard of echoes (or amplifies) the doctrine of exaltation found in the sacred Mormon text, the *Doctrine and Covenants*, in section one hundred and thirty-two, cited above. It is black-and-white, so to speak, and if it were

---

[30] Gerald N. Lund, *Is President Lorenzo Snow's oft-repeated statement—"As man now is, God once was; as God now is, man may be"—accepted as official doctrine by the Church?* (1982); emphasis added.

ever a question in one's mind if it is official Latter-day Saint church doctrine, the article providing the citation above from the year 1982 that is still published to this very day by the Church of Jesus Christ of the Latter-day Saints, says at the very end of the article, "It is clear that the teaching of President Lorenzo Snow is both acceptable and accepted doctrine in the Church today."[31] So the idea and doctrine in Mormonism that men can become gods of their own *worlds* after they die is alive and well, and is continually being taught in Mormonism as a fact of reality. If a Mormon denies the doctrine of exaltation, or the fact that human beings can become gods, then it is presumable that the self-proclaimed Mormon does not yet know what his own sacred Latter-day Saint writings teach.

If there were a question on my use of the word "worlds," above, this no doubt is used in the way Christian apologists have understood it for quite some time. In *Moses (The Pearl of Great Price)* chapter one, verse thirty-three, Heavenly Father says to Moses, "And worlds without number have I created; and I also created them for mine own purpose; and by the Son I created them, which is mine only begotten."[32] In context, this is God speaking to Moses, while they are positioned far beyond the Earth (which is a planet), looking down at "every particle" of the Earth.[33] So the use of the word *"world"* is more accurate according to the Mormon scriptures than the use of the word, *planet*, though they are absolutely talking about the same thing. If a Mormon tried to explain away the doctrine by using the ambiguous word, *world*, it would result in equivocation, because *The Pearl of Great Price* is very specifically talking about planets, as we have seen in context.

To further elaborate on some things recently discussed, a Mormon becomes a god in the Mormon worldview by being married to a wife, even though most Mormons do not discriminate against gender

---

[31] Ibid.

[32] Joseph Smith, *The Pearl of Great Price* (Salt Lake City: The Church of Jesus Christ of Latter-day Saints Intellectual Reserve, Incorporated, 1981), Moses 1:33.

[33] Ibid. Moses, 1:27.

concerning who is eligible to become a god, but interestingly Mormons very rarely discuss *"Heavenly Mother."* But still, many absolutely acknowledge that Heavenly Mother is with Heavenly Father, and therefore claim that women can indirectly become "gods" as well. With this in view, it seems that an inefficient bandage was placed on the rapidly festering wound of sexism. This could likely come from fear of further rejection in society (based on patterns of change in Mormon history and theology; e. g. black people finally being able to enter the priesthood in 1978). Mormonism seems to be making up for past oppression by also mentioning women becoming gods, even though there is no real mention of this in their scriptures. It appears that excuses are being made because there is a complete absence of any mention of Heavenly Mother in Mormon scriptures, but we will discuss this further in chapter three.

Second, the requirement, *"he shall not commit murder"* (which is the case for most people in the history of the world), is easily met. Otherwise, if requirements were too much of a stretch (say, that only *white* men *over* six feet tall, who are married and never murdered anyone and who obey the "law of the Lord" can become gods), then this would clearly reduce the number of people initially attracted to Mormonism severely, since many would not be able to participate in the "glory" mentioned above. So, in order for someone to earn their way to heaven and become gods, the requirements must be easily met, because people would be turned off from the fact of impossibility. The requirements must also exist at all, for the simple fact that many people immediately relate to the requirements and (falsely) see inherent good in themselves.[34] It appears that Joseph Smith learned the secret that people simply appreciate being affirmed in some capacity.

Finally, in order to achieve godhood, one must *"obey the law of the Lord"* according to *Doctrine and Covenants* section one hundred and thirty-two, cited above. As discussed briefly above, this seems to

---

[34] See Ro. 3:23.

be whatever Joseph Smith has written down and is *unquestionably* attributed to being the *word of God* by Mormons. So then, with these three things in play, according to the citation of section one hundred and thirty-two in *Doctrine and Covenants* above, one will *"pass by the angels, and the gods, which are set there, to their Exaltation."* There, they will reach their new destination, where they will be in a state of *eternal progression* (i.e. becoming a god more and more).[35]

So then, from the Mormon perspective, the *reality about God* is that he is an exalted man who once lived on a planet somewhere in the distant universe and lived a morally good life while on that planet, according to the above requirements. When he died, he was resurrected into godhood, and his current status is *eternal progression.* Hence, he is becoming a god more and more.

The claims of the reality about the god in Mormonism can only be *either true or false*, and there are no other alternatives. In logic, this is called the law of excluded middle. This and the following will be discussed in greater detail throughout this book. Either it is the case that God was once a man with flesh and bones, or it is false. Either it is true that this man became more and more glorious and powerful in eternal progression, or it is false. It is either true or false that God came from one of the infinite number of other planets. It is either true or false that infinite regress is even possible (infinite regress is the idea that time goes backwards for eternity and is a requirement for the logical consistency of the doctrine of exaltation). It is either true or false that the one true God has a god over himself. It is either true or false that "as man is, god once was." It is either true or false what the *Doctrine and Covenants* describes about the reality of God. It is either true or false that Mormonism is the one true church under God.

The *reality about man* is in a similar sticky situation. The case for a man in the perspective of Mormonism is that human beings are all

---

[35] Brigham Young. *Teachings of Presidents of the Church.* (Salt Lake City: The Church of Jesus Christ of Latter-day Saints, 1997). Chapter 13. https://www.churchofjesuschrist.org/study/manual/teachings-brigham-young/chapter-13.

potentially gods. This is also either true or false. It is also either true or false that we can earn our salvation. It is either true or false that "*as god is, man may become.*" It is either true or false that mankind has a "Heavenly Mother," let alone a "Heavenly Grandfather." Furthermore, the Mormon doctrine of exaltation is either true or false, and therefore, Mormonism is either true or false. All these things I intend to argue are false in this book, and it all begins with a simple metaphysical, yet childlike question: "Why?"

Metaphysics is the "division of philosophy that is concerned with the fundamental nature of reality and being and that includes ontology, cosmology, and often epistemology."[36] The primary metaphysical focus in this book is cosmological. Cosmology is simply "a branch of metaphysics that deals with the nature of the universe."[37] In other words, cosmological metaphysics will be discussed or alluded to throughout this book, and a major objective is to rule out false teachings and doctrines about the reality of God and his nature and to discover the truth about the reality of His and even man's nature.

The Doctrine of Exaltation Does Not Teach *Why* Men Become Gods

We have discovered the "who" (on several levels), the "what," the "when," etc., but what about the "why?" In a recent conversation where I have asked a Mormon friend, "*Why* is it the case that men become gods?" he tried to explain that the reason that men become gods is because Heavenly Father loves his children (us) so much that he wants the best for us. I explained that this is not even close to what I meant. So, I elaborated,

> Heavenly Father, who was once a man, must have
> inhabited a planet that was at least populated enough

---

[36] Merriam-Webster, *Merriam-Webster's Collegiate Dictionary.* (Springfield, MA: Merriam-Webster, Incorporated, 2003).

[37] Ibid.

to find a wife for himself [because one requirement for obtaining godhood is that he is married]. So, my question is, what is it that makes this possible? Why is it the case that men become gods? If we go back in time for infinity, and all these men through the billions of years become gods, why is it the case? Who or what made this pattern work this way?

At this point, he seemed a bit bewildered, so I took the same conversation to another Latter-day Saint friend of mine. He replied:

One of the beliefs of the Church of Jesus Christ of Latter-day Saints is that through the Atonement of Jesus Christ all humankind has the potential to become perfected and that we can ultimately become like our Father in Heaven. How this is possible is frankly beyond my understanding. It would be certainly interesting to know how or why this has worked this way for eons, but the scriptures do not give us this detail.... I can't imagine this [becoming a god] is an immediate thing that happens. I tend to think of it as a gradual progression over eons and eons. We must prove faithful in this short moment of mortality, and if so, we are granted the opportunity to dwell with God and Christ in the Celestial realms for eternity where we can learn to become like Him. And as we are glorified, it only adds to his glory....

His response is quite revealing on several levels. For one, he admits that this has been going on for "eons." Second, that Mormon scripture has no explanation as to *why* this happens, that men become gods. Third, one does not become a full-fledged god (from the Mormon perspective) in the moment of death. It is a process which takes the same amount of time that men supposedly have been becoming gods: *eons*. Fourth, Mormons are worshiping a mere man. An exalted man, but still a man who likely has not reached his full godhood-ness. Finally, Heavenly Father can have glory added to Him.

Not only is it the case that many Mormons believe that they will one day become a god, but all who do believe in this have a *blind trust* that this will be the case for them. Yet, they never seem to ask the question of "Why?" As we investigate this question of *why*, it will be the case that as we dissect the doctrine of exaltation like a butcher and see what it is really made of, we will not only discover how it supposedly works, but if in fact it works, and if it was ever even alive at all.

In the *Book of Mormon*, there are very few, and even the few are veiled, mentions of the doctrine of exaltation, if one could even consider the few references to be the case. Most of the sources for the doctrine of exaltation are found in the other sacred Mormon scriptures, and even some Mormons with whom I have personally spoken, do not seem to think that the doctrine of exaltation is found in the *Book of Mormon* at all. One of the *Book of Mormon* passages in question is found in Alma chapter thirty-four, verses thirty-two through thirty-four:

> For behold, this life is the time for men to prepare to meet God; yea, behold the day of this life is the day for men to perform their labors. And now, as I said unto you before, as ye have had so many witnesses, therefore, I beseech of you that ye do not procrastinate the day of your repentance until the end; for after this day of life, which is given us to prepare for eternity, behold, if we do not improve our time while in this life, then cometh the night of darkness wherein there can be no labor performed. Ye cannot say, when ye are brought to that awful crisis, that I will repent, that I will return to my God. Nay, ye cannot say this; for that same spirit which doth possess your bodies at the time that ye go out of

this life, that same spirit will have power to possess your body in that eternal world.[38]

This passage is talking about the life that we live in now is essentially a preparation for the chance at being exalted. Also, from this, the reader finds that the doctrine of exaltation is barely found in the "most correct book of any on earth,"[39] which is the description that Joseph Smith himself gave concerning the *Book of Mormon*; the book that he supposedly translated. The official website of the Latter-day Saints does imply that this passage is part of the doctrine of exaltation,[40] which raises some serious questions. First, why is this most foundational doctrine barely found in the *Book of Mormon*? In chapter three, I will encourage people to ask the question of whether or not Exaltation is relevant to one's salvation. Perhaps it is not found in the *Book of Mormon* so much because the *Book of Mormon* is not a deeply theological book, hardly discussing soteriology. Interestingly, it is in the other sacred scriptures of Mormonism where one finds the deeper theology and doctrines such as the doctrine of exaltation. It seems that the reason for this is because the *Book of Mormon* is in a sense, the *face* of Mormonism. They want to put their best foot forward, so to speak, when trying to win converts. This is why they suggest that one should begin his Mormon journey with the *Book of Mormon*, rather than the *Doctrine and Covenants* or the *Pearl of Great Price*.[41] After all, no one does a cannonball into a hot tub. In any case, this *Book of Mormon* passage above seems to be where the doctrine of exaltation

---

[38] *Book of Mormon*, Alma 34:32–34.

[39] Joseph Smith. *History of The Church of Jesus Christ of Latter-day Saints, 7 volumes, edited by Brigham H. Roberts* (Salt Lake City: Deseret Book, 1957), 4:461.

[40] The Church of Jesus Christ of Latter-day Saints. *Gospel Principles*. (Salt Lake City: Intellectual Reserve, Incorporated, 2011). https://churchofjesuschrist.org/study/manual/gospel-principles/chapter-47-Exaltation. Chapter 47.

[41] Similarly (and not as strangely as one may think) with Islam. One does not begin his journey into Islam through the *Hadiths*, but through the *Quran*.

originates, at least in one's supposed path through Mormonism, even if the applied meaning of this passage is an afterthought from the production of the *Doctrine and Covenants*.

I have already mentioned several passages in the *Doctrine and Covenants* that concern the doctrine of exaltation, so now I will only briefly go over them where necessary. It also does not seem necessary to go through them chronologically, since the official Mormon documents and sacred writings are filled with the idea of the doctrine of exaltation, with the exception of the *Book of Mormon* as discussed above.

Please also remember what Joseph Smith was once recorded saying: *"God himself was once as we are now, and is an exalted man, and sits enthroned in yonder heavens!"*[42] This also blatantly teaches that the reality about Heavenly Father is that he was once a man. Heavenly Father was a man, *as we are now*.[43] This is how the doctrine of exaltation plays out in the beginning of a Mormon's life. The idea is inescapable in Mormonism. From this, one can conclude that Mormons literally (and often admittedly) worship a man and are not only okay with it, but that they are good with it, likely because it coheres with many other Latter-day Saint beliefs.[44] This brings up several issues which will be discussed in chapter four.

Sacred, yet Corrupted Holy Scripture

Often a Mormon communicates the idea that the Bible has been corrupted. In the Mormon *Articles of Faith*, one reads, "We believe the Bible to be the word of God as far as it is translated correctly; we

---

[42] Joseph Smith. *Scriptural Teachings of the Prophet Joseph Smith*, 345. https://scriptures.byu.edu/stpjs.html. Italics in original.

[43] This phrase from Joseph Smith is repeated throughout this book to show that the requirements for a man to become a god were also the requirements for Heavenly Father to become a god.

[44] A set of truth claims that cohere with one another can disagree with a different set of truth claims that cohere with one another resulting in contradictions. Therefore, the coherence theory of truth is not logical outside of its own bubble.

also believe the *Book of Mormon* to be the word of God."[45] Notice the qualifying clarification in the phrase *"as far as it is translated correctly."* In First Nephi chapter thirteen, verses twenty-three through twenty-six, one reads:

> And he said: Behold it proceedeth out of the mouth of a Jew. And I, Nephi, beheld it; and he said unto me: The book that thou beholdest is a record of the Jews, which contains the covenants of the Lord, which he hath made unto the house of Israel; and it also containeth many of the prophecies of the holy prophets; and it is a record like unto the engravings which are upon the plates of brass, save there are not so many; nevertheless, they contain the covenants of the Lord, which he hath made unto the house of Israel; wherefore, they are of great worth unto the Gentiles. And the angel of the Lord said unto me: Thou hast beheld that the book proceeded forth from the mouth of a Jew; and *when it proceeded forth from the mouth of a Jew it contained the fulness of the gospel of the Lord, of whom the twelve apostles bear record*; and they bear record according to the truth which is in the Lamb of God. Wherefore, these things go forth from the Jews in purity unto the Gentiles, according to the truth which is in God. *And after they go forth by the hand of the twelve apostles of the Lamb, from the Jews unto the Gentiles, thou seest the formation of that great and abominable church, which is most abominable above all other churches; for behold, they have taken away from the gospel of the Lamb many parts which are plain*

---

[45] Joseph Smith. *History of the Church of Jesus Christ of Latter-day Saints*: *The Articles of Faith*, Volume 4. (Salt Lake City: Deseret Book, 1957), 535–541.

and most precious; and also many covenants of the Lord have they taken away.[46]

So, it is clear why Mormons believe that the Bible has been cor-rupted.[47] That as soon as it reached the hands of the *gentiles* (i.e. from the Mormon perspective, those who are not Mormons), it became cor-rupted in that the gentiles "*have taken away from the gospel of the Lamb which are plain and most precious; and also many covenants of the Lord they have taken away.*"

Even with the above warning about the corruption of the Bible, Mormons still consider the Bible to be one of their four sacred scriptures (again, "As far as it is translated correctly"). In other words, the Bible is a primary source for Mormons.[48] The idea here, properly understood, is that Christians only have *one* sacred book, but Mormons have *four*, therefore Christians are incomplete in some sense. The Bible, however, in comparison to all other religious texts and contrary to what Joseph Smith says about the *Book of Mormon*, is true. Mormons sometimes assume that the Bible cannot be true because of what Joseph Smith taught about it. Following this issue is that even though the Bible is one of the four sacred texts for Mormons, it never once mentions or teaches anything remotely like the doctrine of exaltation.

A Metaphysical Look at the Law of the Gods by Way of Analogies

What I refer to as the "*Law of the gods*" is the idea that I would like to help the reader fully grasp. It is the doctrine of exaltation which is

---

[46] Joseph Smith. *The Book of Mormon.* 1 Nephi 13:23–26; emphasis added.

[47] It is also noteworthy that Mormons do not seem to accuse Christians (gentiles) of adding to the scriptures, but only taking away from them.

[48] Ezra Taft Benson, Gordon B. Hinckley, and Thomas S. Monson. 1992. *First Presidency Statement on the King James Version of the Bible* (The Church of Jesus Christ of the Latter-day Saints. August 1992). https://www.churchofjesuschrist.org/study/ensign/1992/08/news-of-the-church/first-presidency-statement-on-the-king-james-version-of-the-bible?lang=eng.

the Mormon doctrine that men can become gods of their own worlds (or planets). I think that the Law of the gods is a palatable phrase that puts into perspective and simplifies the doctrine of exaltation. I refer to it as the Law of the gods to point out the necessary metaphysical implications behind the doctrine of exaltation. The Law of the gods speaks to this unwritten law that causes men to become gods in the first place. It is kind of like the laws of logic.... We cannot see them, but we know that they exist. In Mormonism, the reality taught therein is that there exists, like the laws of logic, a law that is set in place that causes men to become gods after they die. As in, this is just fundamentally the way it is from the Mormon perspective, no questions asked.

The Law of the gods works a lot like the law of karma in eastern religions. Karma is the idea that one will get what is coming to himself in the next life, depending on how he lived in his present life. So, the way one chooses to live, if he lives a good life, then he will presumably have a better life the next time he is reincarnated. If one were to live a bad life, as in a life filled with crime and taking advantage of people, etc., then he would be judged to a life that is not as good as what he now has, perhaps becoming a lower lifeform in the animal kingdom, or a very poor person.

The ultimate question arises that who is the one who decides if someone had bad karma or good karma in their entire life? The thing is, there is not anyone who decides the karma judgment scales of one's life in order to cause such a being to be reincarnated into a king or a newt. This law is common in Buddhism, Hinduism, and Jainism, as if it were unquestionable reality, but like all laws, there must be a place where they came from, whether these laws are prescriptive or descriptive. This is the simple idea of *the principle of causality*. "Every finite thing needs a cause."[49] There must be a cause. Every effect has a cause, and the law of karma is an effect. The same is the case with the Law of the

---

[49] Norman Geisler. *Systematic Theology*. (Bloomington: Bethany House Publishers, 2011), 130.

gods in Mormonism. The Law of the gods is an effect, and therefore, it must also have a cause.

The following analogy may be beneficial as well, which will help clarify the Mormon beliefs. An acorn becomes an oak tree if it lives an excellent life. What is meant by this is that if the environment is beneficial to the acorn, and the acorn is not biologically or genetically damaged, it will eventually sprout. A Mormon, if he lives an excellent life (if he is beneficial to his environment, and is not damaged himself with specific sins), supposedly will eventually become a god. Acorns have the potential to become an oak tree, just like a Mormon supposedly has the potential to become a god. An acorn becomes a tree, and that tree produces more acorns just like a Mormon supposedly becomes a god of his world and produces more spirit children who inhabit bodies and become Mormons. An oak tree becomes a producer of many acorns and those acorns become oak trees. Heavenly Father became a god and produced many spirit children.

We know that the acorn becomes an oak tree because God (or from the Mormon perspective, *Heavenly Father*) biologically ordered it to be that way. When an oak tree dies, it no longer produces acorns. But when a Mormon dies, he becomes a god because … why? Who or what ordered it to be that way? The acorn becoming a tree is completed in one system. A system that we can analyze and observe. The acorn becoming a tree never leaves the system that it is in. This set finds itself within the ecosystem. The Mormon leaves his system and enters a new one. The question is "Why?" What is it that pulls him out of one place and sets him in another, not only in this one instance, but in all instances from eternity past?

Doubting the Doctrine of Exaltation

In addition to the sources mentioned in chapter one above, it seems that this is a good place to introduce a verse in *Doctrine and Covenants* in section one hundred and thirty-two, verse thirty-seven, in case there is any doubt about the reality of the existence of the doctrine. It says,

> Abraham received concubines, and they bore him children; and *it was accounted unto him for righteousness*, because they were given unto him, and he abode in my law; as Isaac and also Jacob did none other things than that which they were commanded and because they did none other things than they were commanded, *they have entered into their Exaltation, according to the promises, and sit upon thrones, and are not angels but are gods.*[50]

Two things stand out in this verse. One is that it sharply disagrees with the Bible and says that the reason "it was accounted unto him [Abraham] for righteousness" is because he bore children. "It" in this quote is *the bearing of children*. The Bible, on the contrary, reads in the book of James that "The scripture was fulfilled which saith, Abraham believed God, and it was imputed unto him for righteousness: and he was called the Friend of God."[51] The biblical explanation for Abraham's righteousness is because Abraham had faith. In any case, the *Doctrine and Covenants* citation above should be an enormous red flag in the sense that it contradicts what the Bible (one of their own sacred texts) says here and shows specifically that Heavenly Father and the biblical God are vastly different in nature, but it also leads to another, more relative issue in this verse.

The second thing to stand out in this verse is the black and white teaching of the doctrine of exaltation: *"They have entered into their Exaltation, according to the promises, and sit upon thrones, and are not angels but are gods."* "*They*," as in Abraham and those also mentioned

---

[50] Joseph Smith. *Doctrine and Covenants*; 132:37; emphasis, added.

[51] Jas. 2:23.

in the above citation, are now gods (who gained their righteousness through having children and by getting married). If anyone had a question in his or her mind on whether or not Mormonism actually teaches that men can become gods, this seems to be one of the strongest verses in Mormonism's most sacred of documents that displays such a claim. So here again, one finds the Law of the gods is alive and well within Mormonism, but nowhere in the Mormon scriptures is there an explanation of *why* this law is in effect. I submit to you that this law indeed has a cause, if it is true, which we will further elaborate on in chapter four, and we will also come to understand the implications and effects of this law (if true).

In having several conversations with Mormons, I find that when I ask them about the origins of the doctrine of exaltation, they often mention that this is deep material to think about and that we should instead be thinking of better things, and more productive subject material, such as how to live a good life. This is interesting because as briefly noted above, this is a *red herring*, meaning that it is a distraction from the real argument. But one can see why they would want to distract from such an argument—the doctrine that is in question—because not only is the doctrine of exaltation difficult to wrap one's mind around, but it is also very offensive to Christian thought[52] let alone God Himself.

Some Necessary Implications

If the reality of God is that he were once like us (and even still is in many senses according to Mormon teaching), then it seems safe to assume that the planet that he came from (because remember, Heavenly Father populated planet earth with spirit children and they, too, can grow up to become gods of their own planets), was inhabited by several people as well, which is the most natural way to think concerning this because if he were a man once *as we are now*, then he would have had

---

[52] See the discussion on the Nauvoo Expositor in chapter three.

parents just *as we do now*, and possibly had siblings just *as we do now*. We can assume also that there were more people on this planet because in order to reach godhood, a man must be married, as discussed in the introduction. So, if a man must be married in order to attain godhood (*Exaltation*), and Heavenly Father is a man *as we are now*, then he was married as well (a requirement for Exaltation, and the implied Mormon explanation of Heavenly Mother), which means that there is even a greater number of people inhabiting the planet from which he came. But it does not stop there. No, the woman that Exaltation requires him to marry must have also had parents, if he were to have in-laws *as we do now*. Thus, this number of inhabitants on this distant planet keeps growing. Not only this, but we also have yet to mention grandparents and further ancestors of both Heavenly Father and his wife (and even *their physical children* while they inhabited that planet). So, the world from which Heavenly Father came seems very reasonably likened to planet earth in the scientific sense of human inhabitation, but even more so in the description of him being, "*as we are now*," as discussed earlier in this chapter.

The question about Heavenly Father arises about who *his* god was, while living as a man, *as we are now*, on the planet of his birth. (As alluded to in the paragraph above, the question of his birth planet is still up in the air because in the *Pearl of Great Price*, we find in the book of Abraham that "I [Abraham], saw the stars ... And the Lord said unto me: These are the governing ones; and the name of the great one is Kolob, because it is near unto me, for I am the Lord thy God...."[53] So the issue here is that there is some debate between whether Kolob is the planet where Heavenly Father resides, or a star that is near the planet where Heavenly Father resides in the universe.) But, in order for Heavenly Father to be once a man *as we are now*, there also had to be a god over him in order for Heavenly Father to not only exist, but also to become *Heavenly Father*.

---

[53] Joseph Smith, *The Pearl of Great Price*, Abraham 3:2-3.

For all of this to be logically consistent, the whole idea must also consider the question of the number of planets. The planet (or *world*), from where Heavenly Father came must have been created by a different Heavenly Father who came from a different planet. His Heavenly Father came from a different planet, created for him, and this Heavenly Great-grandfather came from a different planet, created for him, and so on, and so on, to infinite regress (eternity past). This idea is implied throughout Mormon scriptures, which will continue to be discussed.

However, at this point, it all goes much further. The questions could also be asked, "Who made it the case that when a person becomes a god, they are to create planets at all? Or create people at all? Or create anything at all? It seems that these ideas and questions could be discussed under another possible chapter titled, *"The Laws for the gods."*

These ideas in Mormon theology require an infinite number of planets, people, gods, and an infinite amount of past time. I have a close—strong Christian—friend who is an ex-Mormon, and in one of our discussions regarding cosmology, he asked me if I have ever studied theories on the multiverse. I confirmed. The conversation quickly died because I said that I do not believe in it because it is just a theory that we will literally never be able to prove or disprove, and because we could take the idea to infinity, which is absurd. It is interesting to note that as a relatively newer Christian, he still deeply believed that the multiverse is true, because either the multiverse or an infinite single universe are the only cosmological models that Mormon theology can consistently operate under. This confirmed for me even further that Mormons typically presuppose an eternal past. Whether one believes in infinite regress of this universe or believes in the multiverse, either case results in an infinite regress of time. The conclusion that one should rightfully make is that if the multiverse or an infinite universe (one of these being that which logically consistent Mormons must hold to) is not true, then Mormon theology cannot be true. I will unpack this in much greater detail in chapter four.

Infinite Worlds

In *The Pearl of Great Price*, again we find more interesting cosmological information. Heavenly Father said to Moses when he was on a high mountain,

> And *worlds without number have I created*; and I also created them for mine own purpose; and by the Son I created them, which is mine only begotten. And the first man of all men have I called Adam, which is many. *But only an account of this earth, and the inhabitants thereof, give I unto you.* For behold, there are many worlds that have passed away by the word of my power. And there are many that now stand, and innumerable are they unto man; but all things are numbered unto me, for they are mine and I know them.... And *as one earth shall pass away, and the heavens thereof even so shall another come*; and there is no end to my works, neither to my words.[54]

From this, the reality that Mormonism describes is that worlds without number have been created. Does this literally mean without number, as in *infinite*? It seems that the answer is that there are always an infinite number of worlds at any given time, but the problem is, that *as one earth shall pass away* (apparently there is more than one earth), *and the heavens thereof even so shall another come*, there is an addition and a subtraction to the infinite set (I will also discuss this in much greater detail in chapter four).

If it did not register yet, we should also give some attention to the idea that there are many earths, from the above citation, and that Heavenly Father is withholding information about the history of the

---

[54] Ibid. Moses 1:33–35, 38; emphasis added.

other earths that both exist in other parts of the universe, and also any earths that have gone on before this one. *"But only an account of this earth, and the inhabitants thereof, give I unto you."* So, the idea that there are other inhabited planets where each one has its own god is unquestionably what Mormon theology teaches. I suppose that if the finite Heavenly Father were to describe the history of the infinite worlds that he had created, it would literally take longer than forever for him to do so. I say this to reveal even more problems with the idea of a finite being becoming infinite, but for now, I digress.

The Metaphysical Pattern: The Child Who Keeps Asking, "Why?"

As one understands this pattern of men becoming gods (the Law of the gods, or the doctrine of exaltation), he finds this law to indeed be in place, but the ultimate metaphysical question is simply, "Why?" As in, if this view of reality about God and the truth of human beings is correct, *why* do men become gods of their own planets? Why is this the case? What is it that set this law into effect? A man grows up and does well and becomes a god after eons of time, as do others also from that same planet, but not only that, others before him and others after him will do the same thing, but *why*?

What is interesting about this Law of the gods is that it *transcends* Mormonism.[55] To *transcend* something means to go beyond the limits or boundaries of something. So, in this sense, as illustrated in the introduction, our perspective needs to transcend what is being described in Mormonism as reality, in order to see that the Law of the gods transcends the gods in Mormonism themselves. The way in which the Law of the gods transcends Mormonism is discussed nowhere in *any* Mormon scripture, which is admitted by many Mormons themselves. The issue here is that Mormons talk about Heavenly Father as if he is the creator of the physical universe, but they also talk about him as if

---

[55] Earlier I mentioned the "Law *for* the gods," which would also transcend all Heavenly Fathers.

he were a man, which results in some serious unanswered questions (One of them being, who or what is it that created the universe or the multiverse?). So what results with Mormons believing the doctrine of exaltation is the kind of faith that Richard Dawkins accuses Christians of having, "blind trust, in the absence of evidence, even in the teeth of evidence."[56] Mormons have a blind trust concerning the Law of the gods (the doctrine of exaltation), because there is nothing that tells them where it comes from, let alone who it came from, why it exists, or how it is possible, and there is nothing higher of an authority than a man who lived for eons, becoming more and more like the god that came before him, so Heavenly Father cannot even know, since he worships his own Heavenly Father. Anyone can see this to be the case because it is indisputably absent from the Mormon scriptures as if Joseph Smith never thought of this becoming a fundamental problem.

Further Basis for the Doctrine of Exaltation

There is a non-profit organization called "*FAIR*," which stands for *Faithful Answers, Informed Response*, and is dedicated to "providing well-documented answers to criticisms of LDS doctrine, belief, and practice."[57] It is a place that combats what Mormon see as an external attack and as false doctrine against the Church of Jesus Christ of the Latter-day Saints' religion. In other words, it is a Mormon apologetics website. In one article, they pose the question: "Do Mormon men

---

[56] Richard Dawkins. *The Selfish Gene, 2nd ed.* (Oxford: Oxford University Press 1989), 198.

[57] Faithful Answers Informed Response. *About* (FAIR: The Foundation for Apologetic Information and Research, 2022). https://www.fairlatterdaysaints.org/about.

believe that they will become 'gods of their own planets and rule over others?'"[58] They answer this by saying the following:

> This isn't just a quibble about semantics. Claims that Mormons hope for "their own planets" almost always aim to disrespect and marginalize, not to understand or clarify. The reality is that we seek eternal life, which we consider to be a life *like* that of our Father in Heaven. We consider our immediate task on Earth to learn to understand and obey the Gospel of Jesus Christ, rather than speculate on what life might be like if we achieve Exaltation. Specifics about the creation of worlds and the ability to govern them upon achieving eternal life are not clarified in Latter-day Saint scripture. Attempts to portray these concepts as simply wanting to "get our own planet" are a mockery of Latter-day Saint beliefs.[59]

They say that the aim of this question is almost always to disrespect and marginalize and not to understand or clarify, but the number one issue is that this is a case of the *poisoning the well* fallacy, because the aim to disrespect and marginalize does not mean that whatever is said following such things is false. Even if a person sets out to disrespect and marginalize Mormons through the doctrine of exaltation yet shows it to be false, does not make the doctrine of exaltation to be true. Sometimes, the truth just hurts. Second, in this case, we are seeking to understand and clarify, and what we conclude from such is that the hope of a Mormon amounts to "getting their own planet."

---

[58] Faithful Answers Informed Response. *Question: Do Mormon men believe that they will become "Gods of their own planets" and rule over others?* (FAIR: The Foundation for Apologetic Information and Research, 2022).

[42]https://www.fairlatterdaysaints.org/answers/Question:_Do_Mormon_men_believe_that_they_will_become_%22gods_of_their_own_planets%22_and_rule_over_others%3F.

[59] Ibid; emphasis added.

FAIR says in the above citation, "The reality is that we seek eternal life, which we consider to be a life like that of our Father in Heaven." Notice here that it also says the word, "like." I find it quite interesting that it also says that "this is not just a quibble about semantics." Again, the idea is that the word *like* does not mean that you should be holy in the sense that God is holy. They do not mean *like* in this sense. As in, live *like* God. There is a small nuance that one should pay close attention to here. What they mean is that a person can become like Heavenly Father in that basically they will one day *be as* him. Not in merely being sanctified, but as in they will have the *same status*. It means, live *as a* god. So, the Mormon view of reality about eternity is that they seek to live an eternal life like Heavenly Father, which simply means *becoming* a god.

In the official website of the Church of Jesus Christ of the Latter-day Saints, we find in *Gospel Principles*, a text that supposedly helps Mormons understand their own doctrine that, "Exaltation is eternal life, the kind of life God lives. He lives in great glory. He is perfect. He possesses all knowledge and all wisdom. He is the Father of spirit children. He is a creator. We can become *like* our Heavenly Father. This is Exaltation."[60] What is interesting about this is the use of the word "*like*" again. Not only does this citation further confirm what we have been discussing even to a greater degree, but also, it again uses the word, "like" in a completely different flavor than what is used when the Bible tells us that we should be holy, [61] or when the Bible says that God made men is His *likeness*.[62] So again, when a Mormon says that one day they will be *like* Heavenly Father, they mean that they will have the same status as Heavenly Father. This is made clear in official Mormon texts, scriptures, articles, and websites. This is the

---

[60] Church of Jesus Christ of the Latter-day Saints. *Gospel Principles*. Chapter 47. https://www.churchofjesuschrist.org/study/manual/gospel-principles/chapter-47-Exaltation?lang=eng; emphasis added.

[61] See 1 Pt. 1:16.

[62] See Gen. 1:26.

reason *FAIR* feels the need to defend themselves. Scrutiny is inevitable regarding such claims.

So then, just because someone *says* that something is a mockery, does not mean that it is. Or, on the other hand, if it *is* a mockery, it does not mean that what is said is false. This is one of the good things about Mormonism, which is that it tends to write everything down, so one can go and see what was once said or described. So, from all these resources, what a person finds in them regarding the doctrine of exaltation is that a man, *if* he is good enough, never murdered anyone, and did not commit adultery more than once ("Thou shalt not commit adultery; and he that committeth adultery, and repenteth not, shall be cast out. But he that has committed adultery and repents with all his heart, and forsaketh it, and doeth it no more, thou shalt forgive; But if he doeth it again, he shall not be forgiven, but shall be cast out"[63]), *then* he will be able to populate his own planet for eternity under the guidance of his own Heavenly Father, while producing more and more Heavenly Fathers *ad infinitum*. This is simply what their scriptures teach, and one can read them and think for himself about what it objectively means.

Summary

The Law of the gods, otherwise known as the doctrine of exaltation, which maintains that any man could become a God if he never murdered anyone and got married while on earth, and also that he did not commit adultery more than once. Hopefully, this doctrine is seen for what it is: a pattern of men working through their lives trying hard to be the best that Heavenly Father calls them to be, with Jesus Christ, the Son of Heavenly Father, helping them earn their place *like* Heavenly Father and rising to become gods of their own planets.

---

[63] Joseph Smith. *Doctrine and Covenants*, 42:24–26.

A key word repeated throughout official Mormon literature is the word, "*like*." As in, all of the children of all Heavenly Fathers in the Mormon view of all existence *may become like* their Heavenly Father, not in the Christian sense of being holy, but in the Mormon sense of becoming one's own Heavenly Father to populate a planet by oneself, bringing his own children up to their own position of Heavenly Father status, which in Mormon doctrine has been happening for eternity past, and will continue for eternity future. This is essentially the *good news* for a Mormon in a nutshell. It seems that in sacrificing one's hope, he instead picks up a burden of impossible work for a poor sense of what Mormonism teaches that heaven should be like.

Chapter Three

Heavenly Father, His Dwelling Place, and His Prophet

> *"A good tree cannot bring forth evil fruit, neither can a corrupt tree bring forth good fruit. Every tree that bringeth not forth good fruit is hewn down, and cast into the fire. Wherefore by their fruits ye shall know them."* ~ Matthew 7:18–20

Getting Down to Brass Tacks: Part Two

THROUGHOUT THE PAGES of this book, I mention some of my investigations and conversations on the held beliefs of individual Mormons. It seems that the question arises, how should we have a conversation about such deep discussion concerning the Mormon doctrine of exaltation? Where does one even begin? Because Christians know the truth, we want our Mormon friends and family to think outside their own box, just like we as Christians want to be able to do the same.

It is good to keep in mind anytime we are witnessing, that we are Christians because Christianity is true. As Christians, we believe that people are Mormons because they are deceived, as with every false religion. To some, this sounds arrogant, but if Christianity is true and

Mormonism is false, then arrogance does not matter. Truth matters. So, how does a person have a conversation with a Mormon regarding the Law of the gods? How can we learn what people believe about the precise nature of Heavenly Father (and indirectly the nature of man) and the doctrine of exaltation? Many of the following questions appropriately overlap in categories, as the reader will discover.

Taking It Easy

As with any spiritually motivated conversation, we want to be cordial and genuine. We are genuine in our quest because we want to learn more about the individual with whom we are speaking. We should be cordial because the Bible tells us in multiple places to be gentle, respectful, use great patience, reason, and careful instruction.[64] After discovering that someone is a Mormon, we might want to start with something simple, such as with easy to answer questions: "How long have you been a Mormon?" or, "What is it that brought you to Mormonism?" This tactic will open doors about being able to discuss what they believe. A reply to questions such as these might be along the lines, of, "I felt in my heart that the Book of Mormon is true." From here you can ask, "How do you feel about the other sacred texts in Mormonism?" If you communicate a genuine interest in the *Doctrine and Covenants*, where the doctrine of exaltation is found, they will instantly be more attracted to the conversation. Mormons seem to love to help curious non-Mormons understand Mormonism.

A Question to Help You Gain Your Friend's Perspective

Begin to go deeper in your quest. You might say, for instance, "Do you consider yourself to be a Latter-day Saint and no other religion?" Ask a question like this because you want to see if your Mormon

---

[64] See 1 Pet. 3:15; 2 Tim. 4:2; Eph. 4:2; 1 Cor. 13:4; Titus 3:2; Prov. 15:1; Jas. 3:17; Phil. 4:5; for a short list of examples.

friend views himself as postmodern thinker. Surprising to some, I have received answers of "no" concerning this question, which was because they claimed to be both Mormon *and* Hindu, or claimed to be both Mormon *and* Muslim, etc. This is precisely the reason for such a question, and it seems always to be clearly well understood when asked. The reason you want to find this out in the beginning of your conversation is because you want to see what you are dealing with for the rest of the conversation. If they are postmodern in their thinking, then that is a whole other issue that needs to be addressed, which we will consider further in chapters five and six. Basically, you want to find out if the person is reasonable, simply because of the Moroni challenge mentioned in chapter one, which again is the challenge about knowing the truth of the *Book of Mormon* from one's heart. The problem here is that our hearts are not the all-encompassing truth detector.

Questions Regarding the Doctrine of Exaltation Directly

Once it is discovered as much as immediately possible how reasonable one is, it is sensible to not waste any time and continue the conversation: "Is it true that we can become like Heavenly Father, an exalted being?" Sometimes Mormons will beat around the bush when asked such things. I believe that the reason there are "noes" to this question is because in any religion, we find people who are at different levels of knowledge within the religion, or they are using a tactic such as *Taqiyya* as discussed in chapter one. That one *can* become like Heavenly Father is absolutely a well-known doctrine within Mormonism, so for one to deny it causes suspicion. This question just puts those in dialogue on the same page. It helps your Mormon friend have a straight answer for such a question, because you are essentially speaking their language and meeting them where they are in such.

If we ask the question, "Is it true that Heavenly Father was once a human being *as we are now*?" we will instantly discover how much, or how little, our Mormon friend knows about his own faith.

My motivation for asking such a question comes from the *Scriptural Teachings of the Prophet Joseph Smith*, and the Lorenzo Snow Couplet, which several of these questions have their inspiration from having the couplet specifically in mind. It is said by a former Mormon that the original motivation for the Lorenzo Snow Couplet (from what is called the King Follett Discourse) is where the Mormon church separated itself from the rest of Christianity, never being able to bring it back.[65] It is indeed the seed of false teaching that grew into the historical Mormon doctrine that distinguished itself from the truth of the gospel.

Questions Concerning the President of the Church

The Lorenzo Snow Couplet again, is: "As man now is, God once was; as God now is, man may become." Before Lorenzo Snow became the fifth President of the Church of the Church of Jesus Christ of Latter-day Saints, he was the President of the Quorum of the Twelve Apostles, which is a group of twelve men selected to operate under the president of the church. Nevertheless, I have heard in some discussions with Mormons that the couplet does not matter much because Lorenzo Snow said it before he was officially the president of the church. One of the main reasons for asking the above question is to see if the person you are speaking with believes that the couplet is truly significant. So, it is good to find out what one thinks of the couplet, whether it is true or false. This will help the discussion continue to move forward.

As mentioned, there may be an objection to the authority of the couplet because they say that Lorenzo Snow was not officially the president of the church when he made this claim. This is also a *red herring*, simply because Mormons presuppose the couplet to be authoritative, based on information from the Latter-day Saints' website. In any event, we can simply follow up with the question, "Is the

---

[65] Matthew Eklund. *The Mormon Chameleon: The Ever-changing Gospel of the LDS Church (Part One).* (Beggars Bread July 2020). https://beggarsbread.org/2020/07/19/the-mormon-chameleon-the-ever-changing-gospel-of-the-lds-church-part-one/.

president of the church a "prophet, seer, and revelator"[66] before or after he becomes president?" I find that most answers to this question are that the president of the church is a prophet *before* he becomes the president. Nevertheless, we want to always keep alert for inconsistencies in the answers to these questions.

In any case, whether people believe or do not believe that he is a prophet before becoming the president, the official website of the Church of Jesus Christ of Latter-day Saints says that the Lorenzo Snow Couplet is official doctrine in the Mormon Church (as cited in chapter one). The negative response to this could also indicate where a Mormon is in his faith journey, or as an idea already briefly discussed, that he is trying to make Mormonism seem more palatable to people he is trying to convert to Mormonism. Unironically, if it is the latter response, it again deeply resembles the doctrine of *Taqiyya* in Islam.

Another question to build on this line of thought could be, "Did Heavenly Father ultimately choose the president of the church, or did human beings? This question is seeking the ultimate giver of authority to the president of the church. If the president receives his authority by human beings, then the Lorenzo Snow Couplet would have less strength, if any at all, because it was simply a human who said it, but if Heavenly Father ultimately chose the president, then the man would begin his path to the presidency on the shoulders of his god. In other words, if Heavenly Father (the supposed one Supreme Being), is the maximally great being, then he cannot be wrong, and this includes anything he says or does. If one answers that human beings ultimately choose the president of the church, then he admittedly adheres to the superiority of man.

---

[66] See *Doctrine and Covenants* 107:91–92.

Questions Regarding the Theology of the Doctrine of Exaltation

Another question to assist in detecting where one is in his Mormon faith journey could be, "Is Heavenly Father absolutely finished in his Exaltation process?" This question seeks to know how Mormons view their Heavenly Father. If they answer in the affirmative, then it usually means that they may not know or have not thoroughly thought through what their scriptures teach. This question indirectly addresses the Latter-day Saint doctrine of *eternal progression*, this again is the idea that Heavenly Father will be forever becoming more and more like his god, basically becoming a better and better being. For those of us who have been a Christian for quite some time, it can still be surprising to hear that many Mormons will answer, "No." The reason this is surprising to a Christian is because if the Mormon god is *not finished* in his Exaltation process, this means that Mormons are comfortable worshiping a mere man (which, this is already clearly understood, but to admit such a thing is logically problematic according to Mormon theology concerning the Supreme Being). I find that in of all these deeper questions for Mormons, this one is the only one where the responses are divided right down the middle. It seems that some believe he is an all-powerful god, and some believe that he is not yet as powerful as he should be. I suspect that the issues are from whether or not the concept of the Supreme Being is in one's mind at the time of the question. The different responses you will likely receive go to show that not all Mormons will fit in the same camp, so to speak. If they confess that they believe what their scriptures teach are true about him being the Supreme Being, then this is an issue of consistency. Either Heavenly Father is the Supreme Being, or he is not yet the Supreme Being. It cannot be both. If they admit that he is not yet the Supreme Being, then this also does not follow according to their own scriptures. Also, if he is not yet the Supreme Being, then he can become greater in degree in some respect, and therefore is not supreme because he is not superior to what he will perhaps one day become.

Something to commit to memory regarding the doctrine of exaltation is the question, "Is Exaltation relevant to our salvation?" Sometimes, as briefly discussed in chapter one, in response to many of these questions, Mormons may tell you that Exaltation is not important, but what is important is *how* one should live. What is meant by this is that instead of being concerned with such things as the deeper thoughts of the doctrine of exaltation, we should be doing good things, being obedient to the laws, and striving to be pure in our daily lives. Unfortunately, as mentioned, for those who try to use this argument, it is a *red herring*. The bottom line is that we want to see if Mormons genuinely regard the doctrine of exaltation as something that they hold to be sacred and worthy of their time to study. From what I have learned in my conversations, it seems that they typically do indeed regard the doctrine of exaltation as relevant to one's salvation, because this is what Mormon salvation ultimately looks like. Exaltation is a result of Mormon salvation, and even more, an end goal. It is also important to note that many brand-new Mormons who are asked this question may not know what Exaltation is, but for a large part, other answers to questions we have discussed may fill in any gaps in information. In any case, a vast majority will claim that it is indeed relevant to salvation when confronted with the importance it has to salvation.

Questions on Mormon Cosmology

When we ask Mormons if there are an infinite number of worlds in the universe, the answer to this question is mostly to help confirm that they have thought about the implications of their beliefs, and that an infinite past is required for Mormonism to remain consistent in their theology. I ask this question to help understand the cosmological beliefs of the Mormons with whom I am speaking. An infinite number of worlds, gods, people, etc., in Mormon cosmology is a requirement for the doctrine of exaltation for several reasons. One of the reasons it must be a requirement is that the Mormon god came from another planet, so *his* god must have come from another planet as well, *ad infinitum*. Not only must there be an infinite number of worlds, but there must also be an infinite number of people inhabiting those infinite number of worlds. With the way all this works, this means that there is also an infinite number of gods. Normally, they will respond that they believe that there are an infinite number of worlds in the universe, and if they do not, as discussed, it is likely that they do not understand or have not studied their own material.

Building on the above question, if Heavenly Father came from one of these worlds, then those who do not believe in an infinite universe will be forced to say "no" in order to remain consistent in their beliefs. But, those who do believe that Heavenly Father came from one of these worlds, think that their god is simply an alien from another planet. Sometimes, you might hear something about the multiverse at this point in the conversation because many people see difficulties in believing in an infinite universe, and so they take it to something more mysterious in their mind so that there will not be any room for objections, but as we will soon see, this is not the case. In the event of either direction, whether they believe that Heavenly Father came from one of these worlds or not, it is likely that 100 percent of Mormons believe that Heavenly Father came from another planet from somewhere, even if it is from another universe because this would all be in line with what the *Doctrine and Covenants* teaches, along with several other documents from the time of Joseph Smith. Needless to say, that from a Christian perspective, this information drives a shocking division between what Christians believe and what Mormons believe about the reality of God.

The Dwelling Place of Heavenly Father

Mormon theology and scripture raise a lot of questions concerning Heavenly Father, certain things that are in proximity to him, and the available information on his whereabouts communicated by Joseph Smith and others. According to another book written by Mormons for Mormons titled, *True to the Faith*, "There are three kingdoms of glory: the celestial kingdom, the terrestrial kingdom, and the telestial kingdom. The glory you inherit will depend on the depth of your conversion, expressed by your obedience to the Lord's commandments. It will depend on the manner in which you have 'received the testimony of Jesus'"[67] What this means is that there are essentially three heavens in Mormonism, and they are at progressing levels of greatness. One reaches the highest heaven, the *celestial kingdom*, by continually living a morally good life while obeying the rules and laws in Mormonism where he will not only populate his own planet with his own spirit children eventually, but also lead them to do the same thing that was done for him, namely, that he became a god because of his Heavenly Father and populated his own planet.

The book elaborates on the celestial kingdom:

> The celestial kingdom is the highest of the three kingdoms of glory. Those in this kingdom will dwell forever in the presence of God the Father and His Son Jesus Christ. *This should be your goal*: to inherit celestial glory and to help others receive that great blessing as well. Such a goal is not achieved in one attempt; it is the result of a lifetime of righteousness and constancy of purpose.[68]

This is the gospel for a Mormon, the "*goal*"; the idea that all doctrines and laws be followed to the "*t*" in order to become gods. It is the hope of mankind in Mormonism even if they play it down, so to speak, when discussing such things.

---

[67] The Church of Jesus Christ of Latter-day Saints. *True to the Faith: A Gospel Reference* (Salt Lake City: Intellectual Reserve, Incorporated. 2004). 92.

[68] Ibid; emphasis added.

What is also interesting in the above citation is that when it says, "Those in this kingdom will dwell forever in the presence of God the Father and His Son Jesus Christ," it does not mean that those who dwell in the celestial kingdom will be on the same planet as Heavenly Father, but it appears to be discussing more of a transcendent place of existence, in the sense that these gods will all have flesh and bones and live on separate planets, but will be able to communicate with the other gods of the other nearby planets, as one would with one's earthly neighbor through something like a telephone or a Zoom meeting. At this point it gets a little confusing, because as briefly mentioned in chapter two, from a reading of the Book of Abraham in the *Pearl of Great Price*, we find that Heavenly Father seems to live on or near Kolob, which appears to be a distant star in the universe:

> And I saw *the stars*, that they were very great, and that *one of them was nearest unto the throne of God*; and there were many great ones which were near into it. And the Lord said unto me: These are the governing ones; and *the name of the great one is Kolob, because it is near unto me*, for I am the Lord thy God: I have set this one to govern all those which belong to the same order as that upon which thou standeth.[69]

So, to know where exactly Heavenly Father resides in the universe is difficult to describe, other than through the Mormon use of what operates like a blanketed term, *"celestial kingdom."* We have discussed the different levels of the Mormon view of heaven (or kingdoms), which, Heavenly Father clearly resides in the celestial kingdom, but to add more confusion, we find the following in *The Pearl of Great Price*:

---

[69] Joseph Smith. *The Pearl of Great Price*. Abraham 3:2–3; emphasis added.

From another revelation to the Prophet Joseph, we learn that *there are three degrees within the celestial kingdom.* To be exalted in the highest degree and continue eternally in family relationships, we must enter into "the new and everlasting covenant of marriage" and be true to that covenant. In other words, temple marriage is a requirement for obtaining the highest degree of celestial glory. All who are worthy to enter into the new and everlasting covenant of marriage will have that opportunity, whether in this life or the next.[70]

The reason even the term *celestial kingdom* is a blanketed term for the Mormon view of heaven is that not only are there three heavens, but there are apparently also three degrees within the *celestial kingdom* itself. In *Doctrine and Covenants* section one hundred and thirty-one, verses one through four, we find even more confirmation on the Mormon concept of what heaven is like, particularly the celestial kingdom, where men become gods. "In the celestial glory there are three heavens or degrees; and in order to obtain the highest, a man must enter into this order of the priesthood [meaning the new and everlasting covenant of marriage]; and if he does not, he cannot obtain it. He may enter into the other, but that is the end of his kingdom; *he cannot have an increase.*"[71]

It is interesting to note here that in *eternal progression*, it is made clear that if he does not reach the highest degree within the celestial kingdom, then he cannot have an increase into the higher degrees. This indicates that one must be in the highest degree of the celestial

---

[70] The Church of Jesus Christ of the Latter-day Saints. *Gospel Topics: Kingdoms of Glory.* https://www.churchofjesuschrist.org/study/manual/gospel-topics/kingdoms-of-glory?lang=eng.; emphasis added.

[71] Joseph Smith. *Doctrine and Covenants.* 131:1–4; brackets in original; emphasis added.

kingdom in order to populate one's own planet with spirit children as a god.[72]

So, the celestial kingdom is the highest of the three "heavens" in Mormonism, which is where Heavenly Father resides. There are three degrees within this kingdom, and it is most frequently understood from the Mormon perspective that Heavenly Father resides in the third, highest degree, but the point of this is that it all results in Mormons worshiping a god who has not yet attained ultimate glory. As in, Heavenly Father is eternally unfinished in his quest for glory. This doctrine (again, *eternal progression*) is the idea that a person will become more and more like his Heavenly Father in eternity. This hard truth results in Mormons, at any level of glory where Heavenly Father resides, worshiping a glorified man who was once a sinner.

Definitions Describing the Nature of Heavenly Father

Worshiping a glorified man reveals several problems, such as with the idea of the word, "supreme" as in, *Supreme Being*. By definition, the Supreme Being is above all other beings in authority and power. But again, Mormons use this word to describe Heavenly Father. I mentioned that I find Mormon beliefs regarding how far Heavenly Father is in his Exaltation process are divided nearly right down the middle. So, about half of the time, Mormons I have asked about this *do not* believe that Heavenly Father is finished progressing (key word is "eternal"), yet none of them will deny his supremacy.

The book mentioned earlier, titled, *True to the Faith*, also mentions the Supreme Being. The first sentence under the section in the book titled, "God the Father" reads: "God the Father is the Supreme Being in whom we believe and whom we worship."[73] This statement is found in their official website, and I would like to show that this is

---

[72] See *Doctrine and Covenants* 132:7, 15–19.

[73] The Church of Jesus Christ of Latter-day Saints. *True to the Faith: A Gospel Reference* (Salt Lake City: Intellectual Reserve, Incorporated. 2004). 92.

a common phrase that Mormons use. The phrase is also found in the *Doctrine and Covenants*, which reads, "But out of respect or reverence to the name of the Supreme Being, to avoid the too frequent repetition of his name, they, the church, in ancient days, called that priesthood after Melchizedek, or the Melchizedek Priesthood." The entirety of this verse is included, but only the description of Heavenly Father as the Supreme Being is what I want to point out. Again, what Joseph Smith has called the most correct book of any on Earth describes Heavenly Father as such: "And Amulek said unto him: Yea, if it be according to the Spirit of the Lord, which is in me; for I shall say nothing which is contrary to the Spirit of the Lord. And Zeezrom said unto him: Behold, here are six onties of silver, and all these will I give thee if thou wilt deny the existence of a Supreme Being."[74] So, here we have three solid examples of the use of the phrase from all different levels of official Mormon scriptures and doctrines that show how common its use is in the Mormon religion.

Another problem is with the word, "eternal," as in Heavenly Father is eternal, or everlasting, or infinite. In the *Book of Mormon*, Mormon chapter nine, verses nine and ten read, "For do we not read that God is the same yesterday, today, and forever, and in him there is no variableness neither shadow of changing? And now, if ye have imagined up unto yourselves a god who doth vary, and in whom there is shadow of changing, then have ye imagined up unto yourselves a god who is not a God of miracles."[75] The idea that Heavenly Father was born as a man, yet is eternal in nature is sewn throughout the fabric of Mormonism:

> By these things we know that there is a God in heaven, who is infinite and eternal, from everlasting to everlasting the same unchangeable God, the framer of heaven and earth, and all things which are in them;

---

[74] *Book of Mormon, Alma* 11:22; see also Alma 12:32 and 30:44.

[75] Joseph Smith. *Book of Mormon.* Mormon 9:9–10.

And that he created man, male and female, after his own image and in his own likeness, created he them; And gave unto them commandments that they should love and serve him, the only living and true God, and that he should be the only being whom they should worship.[76]

Another reading from the *Doctrine and Covenants* says again that Heavenly Father is everlasting to everlasting. "O Lord God Almighty, hear us in these our petitions, and answer us from heaven, thy holy habitation, where thou sittest enthroned, with glory, honor, power, majesty, might, dominion, truth, justice, judgment, mercy, and an infinity of fulness, from everlasting to everlasting."[77] It seems that with all of this, there is a clash between what is said in their scriptures, versus what many Mormons actually believe about their god. Again, in the *Book of Mormon* in Moroni chapter eight, verse eighteen, we find, "For I know that God is not a partial God, neither a changeable being; but he is unchangeable from all eternity to all eternity."[78] So of everything discussed in this so far, which is it? Was Heavenly Father born a human man or is he unchangeable from all eternity to all eternity?[79] Because it clearly cannot be both according to the law of non-contradiction.

The word, *omniscience* (all-knowing), is another example of Mormons not using words as they are classically understood. In Second Nephi chapter two, verse twenty-four, we find that "All things have been

---

[76] Joseph Smith. *Doctrine and Covenants.* 20:17–19.

[77] Ibid. 109:77.

[78] Joseph Smith. *Book of Mormon.* Moroni 8:18.

[79] I have recently discovered from a friend who is a former Mormon that this unchangeableness refers to the material that Heavenly Father is made of, as in, the matter is eternal, and just unformed until Heavenly Father forms the material. But even if the parts of say, a ship are rearranged, during the rearrangement, it is not "unchangeable." Same with a man at death.

done in the wisdom of him who knoweth all things."[80] So apparently Heavenly Father knows all things, but how did that happen if he were born as a human being, *as we are now*? He must have learned all things in eternity since it seems that he had enough time to read every book ever written. But this presents an absurd problem. The problem is that being born a man and having or obtaining omniscience seems to be yet another impossibility. For everything that a person learns, once he learned everything, more information is being produced while he was learning, which would then also have to be learned. While he was learning the information that he missed while he was busy learning, he misses learning the information that was being produced while he was learning the information that he missed earlier, *ad infinitum*.

Also in the *Book of Mormon*, we find further descriptions of an omniscient Heavenly Father: "For behold, God knowing all things, being from everlasting to everlasting, behold, he sent angels to minister unto the children of men, to make manifest concerning the coming of Christ; and in Christ there should come every good thing."[81] This list of passages in Mormon scriptures is far from exhaustive, but it is clear that from these, there is an absolute contradiction in the fact that Heavenly Father is omniscient but also was once a man.

On the Contrary

The Holy Bible, which again, happens to be one of Mormonism's primary sacred sources,[82] does not at all agree with these extremely weak views of supremacy, eternity, and omniscience. For instance, Psalms chapter ninety, verse two says, "Before the mountains were brought forth, or ever thou hadst formed the earth and the world, even

---

[80] Ibid. 2 Nephi 2:24.

[81] Ibid. Moroni 7:22.

[82] Gospel Media. *Do Latter-day Saints Believe in the Bible?* (The Church of Jesus Christ of the Latter-day Saints, 2019). https://www.churchofjesuschrist.org/media/video/2019-07-0020-the-holy-bible-a-witness-of-jesus-christ.

from everlasting to everlasting, thou art God."[83] Again, we find in Psalm chapter ninety-three, verse two, "Thy throne is established of old: thou art from everlasting."[84] In Isaiah one reads, "Hast thou not known? Hast thou not heard, that the everlasting God, the LORD, the Creator of the ends of the earth, fainteth not, neither is weary? There is no searching of his understanding."[85] The Bible continues telling its readers about the eternal nature of God, "For thus saith the high and lofty One that inhabiteth eternity, whose name is Holy; I dwell in the high and holy place...."[86] The one who inhabits eternity must have already been there, which is what John chapter one, verses one through three discusses: "In the beginning was the Word, and the Word was with God, and the Word was God. The same was in the beginning with God. All things were made by him; and without him was not any thing made that was made."[87] What this means is that Jesus was with God the Father, this Supreme Being who the Psalmists and Isaiah discuss. He was with God in the beginning, meaning, before the universe was created. The *Word* already existed, because he (Jesus) is God. So, this is something that definitely does not agree with what Mormon theology teaches. Many Mormons claim that this is talking about the pre-existence of spirit children before these children of God had actual, physical bodies on planet earth. In any case, then, none of these verses understand the concept of the word "supreme" the way that Mormon theology teaches, and similarly, none of these verses agree with the Mormon idea of the word "eternal." Because Heavenly Father, as we have seen, began his life as a created child. Yet, in all this, the Bible is considered one of the four sacred texts of Mormonism.

---

[83] Ps. 90:2.

[84] Ps. 93:2.

[85] Isa. 40:28.

[86] Isa. 57:15.

[87] Jn. 1:1–3.

As far as the God of the Bible being "omniscient" is concerned, there are several verses which discuss the knowledge of God. In Jeremiah chapter one, verse five, we find that God knows Jeremiah before he was even formed in the womb.[88] In Psalms chapter one hundred and thirty-nine, the Psalmist writes about God knowing the words that are on the author's tongue before he even utters them.[89] Again, in the New Testament, we find the same descriptions about *Jesus, who is God in the flesh*: "He saith unto him the third time, 'Simon, son of Jonas, lovest thou me?' Peter was grieved because he said unto him the third time, 'Lovest thou me?' And he said unto him, 'Lord, thou knowest all things; thou knowest that I love thee.' Jesus saith unto him, 'Feed my sheep.'"[90] So the entire Bible is consistent about describing God, from the Old Testament to the New Testament, but this is not the case with the Mormon scriptures. Heavenly Father was born a human man, *as we are now*, so omniscience by his nature is impossible. For instance, how could he possibly have all knowledge about his own birth? Even if he had all the time in the universe to learn about it, he would have to have been there to witness it (which is absurd), but even then, this would not give all knowledge about his own birth. The difference is that God's thoughts are above our thoughts because he was never a man: "'For my thoughts are not your thoughts, neither are your ways my ways,' saith the LORD. 'For as the heavens are higher than the earth, so are my ways higher than your ways, and my thoughts than your thoughts.'"[91] Isaiah clearly describes a different kind of being than what the "three other Mormon scriptures" describe.

Speaking of the nature of God, if one were to read through the book of Numbers, he would find in chapter twenty-three that God is not a man. This same God who is from everlasting to everlasting. "God is

---

[88] See Jer. 1:5.

[89] See Ps. 139:4.

[90] Jn. 21:17.

[91] Isa. 55:8–9.

not a man, that he should lie; neither the son of man, that he should repent: hath he said, and shall he not do it? Or hath he spoken, and shall he not make it good?"[92] On top of that, this same verse clarifies that God is not a son of man (unlike Heavenly Father). God does not change His mind like a man because God is not a man.[93]

In John chapter four, we find that Jesus is talking with the woman at the well, and she saw something that was very different with this man before her, which is interesting because she was apparently very familiar with men, but the reason she sees that Jesus is different is because he told her about these men with whom she was quite familiar.

> The woman saith unto him, Sir, I perceive that thou art a prophet. Our fathers worshipped in this mountain; and ye say, that in Jerusalem is the place where men ought to worship. Jesus saith unto her, Woman, believe me, the hour cometh, when ye shall neither in this mountain, nor yet at Jerusalem, worship the Father. Ye worship ye know not what: we know what we worship: for salvation is of the Jews. But the hour cometh, and now is, when the true worshippers shall worship the Father in spirit and in truth: for the Father seeketh such to worship him. god is a Spirit: and they that worship him must worship him in spirit and in truth.[94]

It is noteworthy that Jesus teaches her several things voluntarily, since she did not even inquire about the nature of God. But more importantly, at least for our current purposes, is that this passage tells us that *God is spirit, and His worshipers must worship Him in spirit and in truth*. This does not sound like the description that Mormonism gives

---

[92] Num. 23:19.

[93] It seems good at this point to again remind the reader that the Bible is a primary source for Mormonism.

[94] Jn. 4:19–24.

about Heavenly Father at all. In fact, it seems the opposite description. Heavenly Father, as we have already discovered in chapter two is *a human man of flesh and bones*, even right now, after what has likely been eons of his eternal progression. As discussed, the issue with this is that these two different descriptions of God violate the law of non-contradiction. It is also the case that the reality about God is either that he has flesh and bones, or that from everlasting to everlasting, he is God, according to the law of excluded middle.

According to relationships with, and even knowledge of other gods, the Bible says, "before me there was no God formed, neither shall there be after me. I, even I, am the LORD; and beside me there is no saviour."[95] Of all beings who would know if there were other gods, would not *the* Supreme Being? Would he be God if there were something he did not know? The Bible is clear on this in several places: "Thus saith the LORD the King of Israel, and his redeemer the LORD of hosts; I am the first, and I am the last; and beside me there is no God.'"[96] Deuteronomy chapter four, verse thirty-five says, "Unto thee it was shewed, that thou mightest know that the LORD he is God; there is none else beside him."[97] This is what I mean when I allude to the idea that Mormons do not understand what the words "supreme" or "eternal" means. They say these words and use them to describe their god, but they are ultimately using them as one would use the word, "*powerful*," which can be used to describe nearly everything in relation to something else. For instance, I am more powerful than someone who can only bench press half of the weight that I can, but what does that matter in light of omnipotence? What is the significance in the power of Heavenly Father, if there are gods more powerful than he, such as *his* Heavenly Father? Ultimately it means that Heavenly Father is not all-powerful. He is not the Supreme Being. The other issue is that there

---

[95] Isa. 43:10–11.

[96] Isa. 44:6.

[97] Dt. 4:35.

is an All-powerful Being, who is the Supreme Being, and this Supreme Being is the God of the Bible, in which Jesus informs us of such.

Again, the Bible is one of the primary sources of Mormonism, yet it flat out disagrees with what is taught in their other sacred texts. The problem is that the different descriptions sound like they are saying the same thing about the two very different deities, because even the Mormon documents are confused and completely disagree in their descriptions about Heavenly Father.

The Person of Joseph Smith

It seems like we can discern at least partially, what kind of a person Joseph Smith was, from the things which he did, taught, and suggests. Remember that Heavenly Father's nature, existence, and his dwelling place are communicated only through Joseph Smith. Jesus says, "The light of the body is the eye: if therefore thine eye be single, thy whole body shall be full of light. But if thine eye be evil, thy whole body shall be full of darkness. If therefore the light that is in thee be darkness, how great is that darkness!"[98] Again, Jesus says,

> Beware of false prophets, which come to you in sheep's clothing, but inwardly they are ravening wolves. Ye shall know them by their fruits. Do men gather grapes of thorns, or figs of thistles? Even so every good tree bringeth forth good fruit; but a corrupt tree bringeth forth evil fruit. A good tree cannot bring forth evil fruit, neither can a corrupt tree bring forth good fruit. Every tree that bringeth not forth good fruit is hewn down, and cast into the fire. Wherefore by their fruits ye shall know them.[99]

---

[98] Mt. 6:22–23.

[99] Mt. 7:15–20.

Perhaps noticing a pattern of the fruits from this man will tell us something about him.

Think of the question, "What is it that drives us as human beings?" We view the world through a particular lens, some of us defining it as we search for truth and others seem to view the world without searching hard at all. What are the answers to the big questions in life: Where did we come from? What is my purpose in life? What happens when we die (et al.)? It seems that the way Joseph Smith viewed the world can be answered by taking a peek into his short time here on earth.

It appears that he had some strange beliefs about where we come from. Consider the following teaching about Heavenly Father:

> We have imagined and supposed that God was God from all eternity. I will refute that idea, and take away the veil, so that you may see. These are incomprehensible ideas to some, but they are simple. *It is the first principle of the Gospel to know for a certainty the Character of God, and to know that we may converse with him as one man converses with another, and that he was once a man like us; yea, that God the Father of us all, dwelt on an earth, the same as Jesus Christ himself did, and I will show it from the Bible.*[100]

Joseph Smith teaches that Heavenly Father was once a man like us and "dwelt on *an* earth." So, in the mind of Joseph Smith, there is an infinite number of planets out there, because there must be an infinite number of gods populating them. In order for Smith's idea to work, there has to be an infinite number of gods populating an infinite number of planets, from an infinite amount of time in the past. These things will be dissected in the next chapter.

---

[100] Joseph Smith, *Teachings of the Prophet Joseph Smith.* 345–346.

Joseph Smith teaching these things should raise some red flags. Just as C. S. Lewis describes possible truths about Jesus,[101] Joseph Smith can in a similar manner, only be a liar, a lunatic, or who he says he is, which is a prophet of God.

There are several more questions which must be raised, however. For instance, a prophet of God would likely not be inspired to translate a *word of God* into a language that was not spoken at the time of the interpretation. The *Book of Mormon* was supposedly translated into *Early Modern English* (i.e. the language of the *King James Version* of the Bible and plays and such written by William Shakespeare), which was not spoken for over two hundred years before the time of the translation of the *Book of Mormon*. If God spoke to Americans, why would He use a language that was not used in common speech? No other prophet in biblical history did anything like this. Smith clearly had presuppositions about this type of language, that it was *holier* than the common language.

Joseph Smith also had several wives.[102] Perhaps this was his motivation to start Mormonism in the first place, because he was simply a sex addict. Think about all of the people who opposed Joseph Smith. He was booted out of places, and they regarded him as a liar themselves. For what reasons? The same reasons anyone would, because they saw that he was seeking only to serve his own sexual desires.

Joseph Smith died in a gunfight, and it seems that prophets of God, as many of them became martyrs, would not be shooting back, especially concerning persecution (if guns existed at the times of the biblical prophets) if they really trusted in and knew God. If Joseph Smith really were a prophet about to get martyred, would he not accept his fate? Consider what Polycarp, the disciple of John, the Apostle of Jesus, said when he was about to be burned alive in the ancient

---

[101]C. S. Lewis. *Mere Christianity* (New York: HarperCollins Publishers, 1996) 52.

[102]The Church of Jesus Christ of the Latter-day Saints. *Gospel Topics Essays: Plural marriage in Kirtland and Nauvoo.* https://www.churchofjesuschrist.org/study/manual/gospel-topics-essays/plural-marriage-in-kirtland-and-nauvoo?lang=eng.

text, the *Martyrdom of Polycarp*: "I give Thee thanks that Thou hast counted me worthy of this day and this hour, that I should have a part in the number of Thy martyrs."[103] In Stark contrast, we find a history of Joseph Smith's death written by the eighth governor of Illinois:

> An attempt was made to break open the door but Joe Smith being armed with a six barrelled pistol furnished by his friends fired several times as the door was bursted open and wounded three of the assailants. At the same time several shots were fired into the room by some of which John Taylor received four wounds and Hiram Smith [Joseph's brother] was instantly killed. Joe Smith now attempted to escape by jumping out of the second story window, but the fall so stunned him that he was unable to rise and being placed in a sitting posture by the conspirators below they despatched him with four balls shot through his body.[104]

So, Smith shot people up and stole men's wives. He made a wrong-era language translation of a book that has no archaeological evidence to support it whatsoever. He taught radical doctrines and teachings never heard of before in nineteen centuries worth of theology, and the list goes on. It seems that the reason Mormonism grew is because he was the type of man who had an answer for everything, and he was better than most at keeping track of his lies. Unfortunately for Mormonism, Smith couldn't keep track of all of his lies, and eventually

---

[103] Alexander Roberts, James Donaldson, and A. Cleveland Coxe, eds., *"The Encyclical Epistle of the Church at Smyrna," in The Apostolic Fathers with Justin Martyr and Irenaeus, vol. 1, The Ante-Nicene Fathers* (Buffalo, NY: Christian Literature Company, 1885), 42.

[104] Governor Thomas Ford. *History of Illinois from its commencement as a state in 1818 TO 1847* (Chicago: SC GRIGGS & CO 1854), 354. http://livinghistoryofillinois.com/pdf_files/History%20of%20Illinois%20from%20it%27s%20Commencement%20as%20a%20State%20in%201814%20to%201847.pdf

they caught up with him and an angry mob exterminated him. It is only Smith's successors who continued to elevate him to a higher status, because they likely also saw the benefits of Mormonism, which was being able to justify the desires of their similar lack of self-control.

Joseph Smith took notice of the trusting naivety of his contemporary fellow man, and through manipulation, convinced a handful of them that he was more than just a storyteller in order to get what he wanted. He was living according to his worldview, which was whatever he desired, because nothing mattered in his eyes. To him, it seemed that there were no gods to answer to, no judges to face, and thus, he manipulated the world around him to do what he did best, to selfishly use people in order to rise in power and to selfishly use women as objects of pleasure.

Mormonism seems to be specifically a man's religion, much like Islam. It all points toward endless sex for the Muslim. But what about Muslim women? What kind of paradise do women get? To share one husband among a crowd of women? It seems like it would get old (among other things) for a woman to share her husband with seventy-two other brides after the first few thousand millennia.

Mormonism is not far from this. Remember that when you die (if you are a good-enough Mormon man), you can populate your own planet with endless celestial sex, in the same way Mormons teach that Heavenly Father has done on *this* planet. Again, what about women? Mere objects. Objects that their husbands supposedly love, but nonetheless, objects. What do women have to look forward to in Mormon eternity? Objectification: Baby machines.

Does it not seem to be a huge red flag that Heavenly Mother is never mentioned in Mormonism's four sacred texts? I was told by a Mormon friend that the reason she is never mentioned, is because human men do not like people talking about their wives, and so one absolutely does not want to talk about Heavenly Mother. This just seems ridiculous because, like nearly all husbands worth their salt, I am extremely protective of my family and personally have no problem with people talking about my wife. Anytime someone says anything about her it is positive because she is an amazing woman. I am certain that I am not the only husband in the world who thinks like this. Even the Mormon fellow who told me this does not mind me asking how his wife is doing.

Joseph Smith clearly did not have a healthy fear that he would have to answer for these kinds of things. In the book of James, chapter three, the Bible teaches us that not many of us should become teachers because teachers will receive a harsher judgment.[105] If Smith read this (which most Mormons believe he was at minimum, a biblical scholar), then he would know that if he taught things were which were wrong, he would receive harsher judgment. Otherwise, we have reason to believe that if he read James, he did not believe anything it said. Teachers receive harsher judgment because by teaching they claim to be somewhat of an expert on what they teach. If one teaches theology or doctrine then he claims to have expertise on the subject. The fact that Joseph Smith taught enormous amounts of doctrine that clearly disagrees with what the Bible teaches, he is claiming to be an authority on theology (through revelation), at the least. Let alone an authority that is higher than the Bible. As such, we can conclude that he either doesn't *care* what the Bible says, which, through the eyes of Pascal, would be a seriously uneven wager, or that he doesn't *believe* what the Bible says, which would make him a liar or a lunatic. Lacking morality and manipulating those around him to feed his sexual desire, brings a conclusion that Smith did not believe that he must answer to a Just Judge.

As mentioned, in the trilemma that C.S. Lewis offers his readers in *Mere Christianity* about Jesus, there are three choices: liar, lunatic or Lord. And because of His miracles, because of the things that the apostles said of Him, and because they died for what they kept saying of the Lord, we can conclude that Jesus is Lord. Joseph Smith, on

---

[105]See Jas. 3:1.

the other hand, was probably not a lunatic; after all, he could clearly formulate complicated, premeditated thoughts. He was not a prophet because of the reasons listed above (and a plethora of other reasons), but he was a liar. Why? Because he had the disease that is pandemic to human beings: He wanted to serve himself.

The Nauvoo Expositor

From *The Nauvoo Expositor*, one can see that in the earliest resources by Mormons that there were some issues with the doctrine of exaltation, "right off the bat," so to speak. The *Nauvoo Expositor* was a newspaper that only ever had one issue. After the first issue was printed, Joseph Smith had the printing press burned down to the ground because he did not like what was published about him. In the Brigham Young University Encyclopedia, the following statement is made about the Nauvoo Expositor:

> The Nauvoo Expositor was the newspaper voice of apostates determined to destroy the Prophet Joseph Smith and the Church of Jesus Christ of Latter-day Saints in the spring of 1844. During the last few months of Joseph Smith's life, an opposition party of disgruntled members, apostates, and excommunicants coalesced into a dissenting church. *The principals claimed to believe in the Book of Mormon and the restoration of the gospel, but rejected what they termed Nauvoo innovations, notably plural marriage....*
>
> Nauvoo residents were incensed at what they saw as its sensational, yellow-journalistic claims about Nauvoo religion, politics, and morality. They were also struck with sharp foreboding. Francis Higbee, one of the proprietors of the newspaper, set an ominous tone

when he described Joseph Smith as "the biggest villain that goes unhung...."

As mayor of Nauvoo, Joseph Smith summoned the city council. Following fourteen hours of deliberation in three different sessions, the council resolved on Monday, June 10, about 6:30 p.m., that the newspaper and its printing office were "a public nuisance" and instructed the mayor "to remove it without delay." Joseph Smith promptly ordered the city marshal to destroy the press and burn all copies of the paper. At 8:00 p.m. the marshal carried out the mayor's orders (HC 6:432-49).[106]

Polygamy definitely has its place of discussion, but our focus is on the doctrine of exaltation, which was clearly an issue, even with people who self-identified as Mormons early on. So then, as the mayor of Nauvoo, Joseph Smith had the whole printing press burned down because he did not like what they said about his teaching of "the restoration of the gospel" and plural marriage. What is meant by the "restoration of the gospel" in this text is the exact thing we have been discussing all along: the doctrine of exaltation, or again, what I like to refer to as the Law of the gods.

The first issue of the Nauvoo Expositor can still be found throughout the internet because there seemed to be decent circulation of it at the time and people likely kept their copies for safe keeping, which makes the only issue ever printed by the Expositor available to the world through numerous PDF files of it which can easily be found because they are now Public Domain. Two portions of the Nauvoo

---

[106]Daniel H. Ludlow, *Encyclopedia of Mormonism: the history, scripture, doctrine and procedure of the Church of Jesus Christ of the Latter-day Saints* (New York: Macmillan Publishing Company, 1992). Nauvoo Expositor; https://contentdm.lib. byu.edu/digital/collection/EoM/id/3984; emphasis added.

Expositor seem to be especially noteworthy for our purposes. The first citation reads,

> We all verily believe, and many of us know of a surety, that the religion of the Latter Day Saints, as originally taught by Joseph Smith, which is contained in the Old and New Testaments, Book of Covenants, and *Book of Mormon*, is Verily true; and that the pure principles set forth in those books, are the immutable and eternal principles of Heaven, and speaks a language which, when spoken in truth and virtue, sinks deep into the heart of every honest man.— Its precepts are invigorating, and in every sense of the word, tend to dignify and ennoble man's conceptions of God and his attributes.[107]

This states clearly that these are people who considered themselves to be Mormons, and they even list all of the sacred books of the Mormon faith with the exception of the *Pearl of Great Price*. All of this took place in the forty-fourth year of the nineteenth century. The *Pearl of Great Price* was written approximately seven years later which explains the lack of mentioning such. The "Book of Covenants" that is mentioned in the citation is what is now known as the *Doctrine and Covenants*, which is where most of the theology is found regarding the doctrine of exaltation. So, the Nauvoo Expositor praised Joseph Smith at least in some sense still, and the journalists therein even considered themselves to be Mormons.

A second citation that is noteworthy is the following:

> *Among the many items of false doctrine that are taught*
> *the Church, is the doctrine of many Gods, one of the*

---

[107]Nauvoo Expositor. Public Domain. https://archive.org/details/Nauvoo Expositor1844.

most direful in its effects that has characterized the world, for many centuries. We know not what to call it other than blasphemy, for it is most unquestionably, speaking of God in an impious and irreverent manner.— It is contended that there are innumerable Gods as much above the God that presides over this universe, as he is above us; and if he varies from the law unto which he is subjected, he, with all his creatures, will be cast down as was Lucifer....[108]

This seem to show that Mormonism did not teach the doctrine of exaltation early on in its history, or that, again, people who were Mormons did not get that far in their Mormon journey. Simply because those who wrote the content for the Nauvoo Expositor did not know about the doctrine of exaltation when they became Mormons. In any case, then, there is still no question of whether Mormonism teaches this doctrine in its theology now, even though it came as a surprise to these early witnesses. Not only this, but we have literal evidence of people early in the history of the Church of Jesus Christ of the Latter-day Saints who claimed to be Mormon, combatting the doctrine of exaltation.

Joseph Smith Had the Same Demon that Influenced Muhammad

In chapter one, I briefly alluded to the fact that Mormonism is a result of the work of the devil, and it seems that a good way to see the truth of this is through a comparison with Islam. In an apologetics class to Islam, as I was reading through the textbooks and material, and already being well versed in Mormon history and theology, I could not help but notice such extreme familiarity between Islam and Mormonism. But what does Islam have in common with Mormonism?

---

[108]Ibid. Emphasis added.

The similarities are uncanny. Like human beings, *demons are creatures of habit*. The Bible does not tell us much about them, but from what it does tell us, we can gather valuable information. Jesus reveals to us some things about their behavior:

> When the unclean spirit is gone out of a man, he walketh through dry places, seeking rest, and findeth none. Then he saith, I will return into my house from whence I came out; and when he is come, he findeth it empty, swept, and garnished. Then goeth he, and taketh with himself seven other spirits more wicked than himself, and they enter in and dwell there: and the last state of that man is worse than the first. Even so shall it be also unto this wicked generation....[109]

Jesus clearly understands that demons have typical behaviors. He has seen it many times before. He lets us know that a typical behavior for a demon is that *home is where the heart is*. When one's house crumbles to the ground or gets burned in a fire, he moves to a new one. Likewise, when a person dies, the demon is forced to move to a new person. Much like what we are discussing here: moving from Muhammad to Joseph Smith and likely several in between.

I find it interesting what Paul teaches Timothy about where the doctrines or teachings of demons come from: "Now the Spirit speaketh expressly, that in the latter times some shall depart from the faith, giving heed to seducing spirits, and doctrines of devils; Speaking lies in hypocrisy; having their conscience seared with a hot iron...."[110] This passage seems to give strength to the argument that Christians cannot be possessed, but that they can be influenced. I say this because I cannot confirm that Joseph Smith and Muhammad were possessed, but

---

[109]Mt. 12:43-45.

[110]1 Ti. 4:1–2; emphasis added.

I am convinced that they were at least influenced by the same demon. Some may reduce it to simple plagiarism of Islamic practices, but in either case, demonic influence could be present.

Consider another typical experience found in the New Testament Gospels concerning demons. Someone brings a person who is possessed by a demon to Jesus, and at times, there is a wild reaction at the sight of Jesus by the demon, signifying yet another typical behavior, but in the case that the person is blind because of the demon, there seems to be no such reaction: "Then was brought unto him one possessed with a devil, blind, and dumb: and he healed him, insomuch that the blind and dumb both spake and saw."[111] So, with this man who was possessed by a devil (the Greek word used here is δαιμονιζόμενος, which means to be possessed by a demon) and set free by Jesus, it seems to suggest that there was a demon *working* to keep this man blind and mute in an ongoing fashion. In other words, a demon lived in this man and made his house (out of him) the way he liked it, and maintained the furniture in his *house*, so to speak, much like any mere human being would. Another point to this is to show that demons are very comfortable around human beings, perhaps because human beings are also creatures of habit, and so the demon can learn the habits and accommodate. In other words, human beings are predictable. In any case, we find that from these passages, we can conclude that a demon prefers what is familiar and predictable and will manipulate the person he possesses or influences in a specific direction because demons are also creatures of habit.

One way to see that the same demon that influenced (or possessed) Muhammad ultimately landed in Joseph Smith is by examining the tracks that were left in the snow. When an animal has a distinct physical characteristic such as a broken leg that was healed, or a toe that was trapped somehow and pulled off, or even a leg that was stuck in between two trees and the animal broke it off, a tracker can recognize

---

[111] Mt. 12:22.

the distinctions in the tracks and clearly see that he is following this same animal, even from several days or weeks before, for whatever reason (hunting, biological studies, photography, etc.). So, let's now look at the tracks in the snow, so to speak, and we will see that it is the case that the founder of Mormonism was indeed possessed (or influenced) by the same demon as the founder of Islam.

They Both Had Multiple Wives

Sura 4:3 in the Quran, we find, "And if you fear that you cannot act equitably towards orphans, then marry such women as seem good to you, two and three and four; but if you fear that you will not do justice (between them), then (marry) only one or what your right hands possess; this is more proper, that you may not deviate from the right course."[112] Here, not only does this passage in the Quran condone polygamy, but even gives a specific number that a man can marry.

The Latter-day Saints website states, "After receiving a revelation commanding him to practice plural marriage, Joseph Smith married multiple wives and introduced the practice to close associates."[113] Again, we find that, conveniently, Joseph Smith received a revelation and therefore condoned polygamy, at least at first.

It is common knowledge that both the founder of Islam and the founder of Mormonism were deeply rooted in polygamy. Many have argued at this point that the Bible is as well condoning polygamy (here, the reader should recall that the Bible is one of the four sacred books of Mormonism), but the difference is that the Bible never *condones* polygamy, but simply *records* the sinful acts of some of the characters

---

[112]M. H. Shakir, ed., *The Quran* (Medford, MA: Perseus Digital Library, n.d.). Sura 4:3.

[113]The Church of Jesus Christ of the Latter-day Saints. *Church History Topics: Joseph Smith and Plural Marriage.* https://www.churchofjesuschrist.org/study/history/topics/joseph-smith-and-plural-marriage.?lang=eng.

in the Bible, whereas Islam does condone it, and Mormonism did (and many Mormons today still condone it).

Polygamy and polyandry both belittle the opposite sex. Polygamy shows how women are lower than men in importance, and similarly for polyandry, men are belittled by elevating the woman above men in a matter of importance. *The Bible teaches that men and women are equal in importance.*[114] In Galatians, we read, "There is neither Jew nor Greek, there is neither bond nor free, there is neither male nor female: for ye are all one in Christ Jesus."[115] In Christianity, the souls of women and men are held in the same respect. This cannot be said of either Mormonism or Islam.

They Both Claimed to be a Prophet

The Quran tells its readers that "Muhammad is the messenger of Allah...." It is pretty clear that Muhammad thought highly of himself. See the larger context:

> He it is who sent His Messenger with the guidance and the true religion that He may make it prevail over all the religions; and *Allah is enough for a witness. Muhammad is the Messenger of Allah,* and those with him are firm of heart against the unbelievers, compassionate among themselves; you will see them bowing down, prostrating themselves, seeking grace from Allah and pleasure; their marks are in their faces because of the effect of prostration; that is their description in the *Taurat* [Torah] and their description in the *Injeel* [New Testament]; like as seed-produce that puts forth its sprout, then strengthens it, so it becomes stout and

---

[114]*Roles* are a different topic.

[115]See Gal. 3:28.

stands firmly on its stem, delighting the sowers that He may enrage the unbelievers on account of them; Allah has promised those among them who believe and do good, forgiveness and a great reward.[116]

Similarly, Joseph Smith writes, "And again, so soon as I had the spirit of prophecy, when standing up, I prophesied concerning the rise of this Church, and many other things connected with the Church, and this generation of the children of men."[117]

Both Joseph Smith and Muhammad claimed to be prophets of God, and though there are uncanny similarities between the two, there are no similarities between these and biblical prophets.

They Both were Visited by an Angel

One of my former professors describes in his book, the story of what Muslims believe to be the history of how Muhammad received his revelation:

When Muhammad said that he could not read, the angel embraced him and forced the air out of his lungs, and then commanded him again to read. Again, Muhammad said he did not know how to read. This sequence occurred three times before the angel finally told him what the words were on the cloth.

'Proclaim! (or read!) in the name of thy Lord and
Cherisher, Who created-
Created man, out of a (mere) clot of congealed blood:
Proclaim! And thy Lord is Most Bountiful,
Who taught (the use of) the pen,

---

[116]M. H. Shakir, ed., *The Quran*, Sura 48:28–29; emphasis added.

[117]*Joseph Smith—History*. 1:73.

Heavenly Father, His Dwelling Place, and His Prophet

Taught man that which he knew not'

This passage was the first revelation of what has become known as the Quran, which is a term related to the command *to read* or *to recite*.[118]

So, Muhammad clearly claims to have been visited by an angel, but what about Joseph Smith? See if you can spot the same *broken-legged* tracks in the snow. In *The History of Joseph Smith*, which is an *auto-biography*, we find the following:

> While I was thus in the act of calling upon God, I discovered a light appearing in my room, which continued to increase until the room was lighter than at noonday, when immediately a personage appeared at my bedside, standing in the air, for his feet did not touch the floor....
>
> He called me by name, and said unto me that he was a messenger sent from the presence of God to me, and that his name was Moroni; that God had a work for me to do; and that my name should be had for good and evil among all nations, kindreds, and tongues, or that it should be both good and evil spoken of among all people.[119]

Does it show yet that Muhammad and Joseph Smith both fall under something bigger? That there is a *creature of habit* influencing both of them? Let us continue.

---

[118] Daniel Janosik. *The Guide to Answering Islam: What every Christian needs to know about Islam and the rise of radical Islam* (Cambridge: Christian Publishing House, 2019), 23

[119] Joseph Smith. *The Testimony of the Prophet Joseph Smith* (Salt Lake City: Church of Jesus Christ of the Latter-day Saints. 2013). https://www.churchofjesuschrist.org/study/scriptures/bofm/js?lang=ase.

77

They Both Taught about Jesus Differently Than What the Bible Teaches

Even though they both were alive much later than when the Bible was written, they both taught that Jesus was different than what the Bible describes. Look at what the Quran says about Jesus, which was written six hundred years after the time of Jesus:

> And their saying: Surely we have killed the Messiah, Isa son of Marium, the messenger of Allah; and they did not kill him nor did they crucify him, but it appeared to them so (like Isa) and most surely those who differ therein are only in a doubt about it; they have no knowledge respecting it, but only follow a conjecture, and they killed him not for sure. Nay! Allah took him up to Himself; and Allah is Mighty, Wise.[120]

The question is, should we believe a source that was written much later than the event, or would it make more sense to believe a source closer in time to the event? Think about the events of September 11, 2001, for instance. Would journalism be likely more accurate a year after the event or a thousand years after the event, when all the witnesses are dead and there is so much time for embellished legends to begin cropping up? It seems obvious at this point.

When one sees what Joseph Smith taught about Jesus in the *Book of Mormon*, it seems clear that it is a direct, yet twisted plagiarism of the Bible. In Second Nephi, Joseph Smith writes, "For we labor diligently to write, to persuade our children, and also our brethren, to believe in Christ, and to be reconciled to God; for we know that it is by grace we are saved, after all we can do."[121]

---

[120]M. H. Shakir, ed., *The Quran*, Sura 4:171.

[121]Joseph Smith. *Book of Mormon*. 2 Nephi 25:23.

It might sound okay at first reading, but when the *Book of Mormon* says, "to believe in Christ," the question arises, "To which *Christ* is he referring?" in 2 Corinthians 11:4, Paul tells the Corinthians that one of their issues is that they too easily believe in *another Jesus*: "For if he that cometh preacheth *another Jesus*, whom we have not preached, or if ye receive another spirit, which ye have not received, or another gospel, which ye have not accepted, ye might well bear with him."[122] This phrase, *another Jesus*, is often something that Mormons see as absurd, as if the concept does not exist, and they get offended at the suggestion that the Mormon Jesus is different than the biblical Jesus, but here is the possibility of such in black and white. On top of this, how can we pull ourselves up by our own bootstraps? "After all we can do?" How can we help in our own salvation?

In Ephesians chapter two, we find that it is "by grace are ye saved through faith; and that not of yourselves: it is the gift of God: Not of works, lest any man should boast."[123] These two contrary passages have very similar verbiage, yet they describe two very different Saviors. One is like a janitor,[124] sweeping up the mess of moral failures that people leave behind, which ultimately teaches that those who fail morally against God (sin) help reach the goal of their own salvation, and the other (from the Bible) provides salvation purely as a free gift, and there is nothing we (sinners) can do to earn any part of it.

So, the Mormon Jesus or the Muslim Jesus is not the same Jesus that the Bible describes. The law of non-contradiction shows us that not all three of these can be true at the same time and in the same sense. At least two of these (between the Bible, the Quran, and the *Book of Mormon*) *must* be false. I maintain that the biblical account is true, and the *Book of Mormon* and the Quran and what they teach are false.

---

[122] 2 Cor. 11:4; emphasis added.

[123] Eph. 2:8–9.

[124] This analogy is found in Lynn Wilder's book, *Unveiling Grace: The story of how we found our way out of the Mormon Church* (Grand Rapids: Zondervan, 2013). 213.

Both Taught That the Bible Is Corrupted

In order for a new religion such as this to work and for converts to be won over to the new religion, there must be an attack on the Bible itself. The Quran teaches that the Bible is corrupted in several passages. Here below is but one:

> They altered the words from their places and they neglected a portion of what they were reminded of; and you shall always discover treachery in them excepting a few of them; so pardon them and turn away; surely Allah loves those who do good (to others). And with those who say, we are Christians, we made a covenant, but they neglected a portion of what they were reminded of, therefore we excited among them enmity and hatred to the day of resurrection; and Allah will inform them of what they did.[125]

As alluded to, it is a basic requirement for a new theistic religion to attack the Bible's integrity because everyone knows that the law of non-contradiction would shut the new religion down.[126] This is why the Bible's authority must be deeply questioned for new opposing doctrines to be taught.

Similarly, in the *Book of Mormon*, Joseph Smith writes, "For behold, they have taken away from the gospel of the Lamb many parts which are plain and most precious; and also many covenants of the Lord have they taken away."[127] Again, in the "Articles of Faith," Smith writes, "We believe the Bible to be the word of God as far as it

---

[125]M. H. Shakir, ed., *The Quran*, Sura 5:13–14; see also 3:78; 4:46; 2:75–78; et al.

[126]See chapter six for a further discussion on the integrity of the Bible.

[127]Joseph Smith, *Book of Mormon*. 1 Nephi 13:26.

is translated correctly; we also believe the *Book of Mormon* to be the word of God."[128] In the Bible, there is a curse spelled out for those to add or take away from the Bible: "For I testify unto every man that heareth the words of the prophecy of this book, If any man shall add unto these things, God shall add unto him the plagues that are written in this book: And if any man shall take away from the words of the book of this prophecy, God shall take away his part out of the book of life, and out of the holy city, and from the things which are written in this book."[129] Since the *Book of Mormon* came after the Bible, and adds to the prophecy of the Revelation, then the author is cursed.

If the reader were not convinced that Joseph Smith does not add to or take away from the Revelation, perhaps he will be after considering the following: In *Doctrine and Covenants*, the Mormon church says about the *Doctrine and Covenants* that,

> Though there may be those who consider the *Doctrine and Covenants* prophecies pertaining to this last day (D&C 45:42; D&C 64:24) before Christ's coming to the world as mere hyperbole, such is not the case. *There is an undeniable literalness to the Doctrine and Covenants.* Hence, the admonition to "search these commandments, for they are true and faithful, and the prophecies and promises which are in them shall all be fulfilled.[130]

---

[128]The Church of Jesus Christ of the Latter-day Saints. *History of the church*, Vol. 4, pp. 535–541.

[129]Rev. 22:18–19.

[130]Rodney Turner. *Prophecies and Promises of the Doctrine and Covenants.* (The Church of Jesus Christ of the Latter-day Saints, 1972). https://abn.churchofje-suschrist.org/study/ensign/1972/12/prophecies-and-promises-of-the-doc-trine-and-covenants?lang=eng; emphasis added.

So then, we are to take the *Doctrine and Covenants* undeniably literally, according to the above citation. This is not only devastating to the Mormon faith, but also to Joseph Smith himself.

In *Doctrine and Covenants*, section forty-five, we find several things that not only take away from the Revelation of Jesus, but that also add to the Revelation of Jesus in the Bible. For instance, in verses sixty-four through sixty-six in *Doctrine and Covenants*, it reads,

> Wherefore I, the Lord, have said, gather ye out from the eastern lands, assemble ye yourselves together ye elders of my church; go ye forth into the western countries, call upon the inhabitants to repent, and inasmuch as they do repent, build up churches unto me. And with one heart and with one mind, *gather up your riches that ye may purchase an inheritance* which shall hereafter be appointed unto you. *And it shall be called the New Jerusalem*, a land of peace, a city of refuge, a place of safety for the saints of the Most High God....[131]

This is a very different description of the New Jerusalem and how we are to be a part of it than what the book of Revelation says:

> And I saw a new heaven and a new earth: for the first heaven and the first earth were passed away; and there was no more sea. And I John saw the holy city, *new Jerusalem, coming down from God out of heaven, prepared as a bride adorned for her husband.* And I heard a great voice out of heaven saying, Behold, the tabernacle of God is with men, and he will dwell with them, and they shall be his people, and God himself shall be with them, and be their God

---

[131]Joseph Smith, *Doctrine and Covenants*, 45:64-66; emphasis added.

And the Spirit and the bride say, Come. And let him that heareth say, Come. And let him that is athirst come. *And whosoever will, let him take the water of life freely.*[132]

One says that the New Jerusalem is *purchased* through the gathering of riches, and the other says that the New Jerusalem will come down from heaven.[133] The *Doctrine and Covenants*, by saying this, and ultimately, Joseph Smith, both *takes away* from the Revelation *and adds* to it. The reason this is an issue is because in the Revelation, we find the curse mentioned in 22:18–19 above. The description of the objective reality found within the Revelation is not to be changed in any way. But as we can see, this is exactly what the *Doctrine and Covenants* does.

In the first citation from the Latter-day Saints website above, we also find the confession that "The *Doctrine and Covenants* is the only one of the standard works to be produced in modern times."[134] So, this book was produced in modern times, according to the Mormon church. This makes the *Doctrine and Covenants* to obviously come chronologically after the Revelation, and without question takes away from and adds to "the words of the prophecy of this book," speaking of the Revelation itself.

This should cause an uncomfortable stir in the mind of the Mormon. How is this issue dealt with coming from Mormons theologically speaking? Deuteronomy chapter four, verse two, will often be used and abused by a trained Mormon. It says, "Ye shall not add unto the word which I command you, neither shall ye diminish ought from it,

---

[132]Rev. 21:1–3, 22:17; emphasis added.

[133]The point of the New Jerusalem being a bride is because God will be her Husband and will attend to "her."

[134]Rodney Turner. *Prophecies and Promises of the Doctrine and Covenants.* (Salt Lake City: The Church of Jesus Christ of the Latter-day Saints, 1972), Ensign, Volume 2, Number 12.

that ye may keep the commandments of the LORD your God which I command you."[135] Mormons often use this to say that there are more words after this verse, so then basically it doesn't matter. The problem is that this verse is strictly speaking of *commandments*, not of *prophecy*. It should be understood as adding or taking away from the commandments. If it were mere words that were the issue in this verse, then the human author himself would be breaking the law that he just wrote down. So would Joshua, Ruth, Samuel, King David, Matthew, Mark, Luke, John, Paul, etc. The idea that Deuteronomy chapter four, verse two, is a strong argument for the permission that Mormons can add to scripture is absurd. In fact, it fails completely. The Revelation passage above speaks of prophecy, and the Deuteronomy passage speaks of commandments. These are two different subjects entirely.

Since the *Doctrine and Covenants* are admittedly written by Joseph Smith as discussed above, it seems safe to believe that he is cursed with the plagues described in the Revelation, and also that God will take away his share in the tree of life and in the holy city which are described in the Revelation. What does the fruit that Joseph Smith produces tell us about him? What does this say about the rest of the things that he said and did? What do these behaviors tell us about what kind of man was Joseph Smith?

The *Book of Mormon*, because it teaches a different gospel than what the Bible teaches, in fact, different than what the Revelation specifically teaches, can be included in the curse from the Revelation. Take for instance Revelation chapter one, verses five and six, "And from Jesus Christ, who is the faithful witness, and the first begotten of the dead, and the prince of the kings of the earth. Unto him that loved us, and washed us from our sins in his own blood, And hath made us kings and priests unto God and his Father; to him be glory and dominion for ever and ever. Amen."[136] These verses *are* the gospel. The Good News

---

[135]Dt. 4:2.

[136]Rev. 1:5–6.

that people are freed from sin by the blood of Christ. The gospel in the *Book of Mormon* (which is really no gospel at all), is found in Second Nephi, as discussed above, "For we know that it is by grace that we are saved, after all we can do."[137] This is saying something very different than what the gospel in the Revelation says. It is through this that we can also understand how the *Book of Mormon* both adds to and takes away from the Revelation. As far as prophecy is concerned, the entire book of Revelation is prophetic. A prophet is one who speaks the will of God to others. It is in this sense that a prophet can reveal the future through the power of God, which is most of the content of the Revelation, and a prophet can also reveal the will of God by stating what is already known, such as the gospel in Revelation chapter one.[138] When we read Revelation chapter twenty-two, verses eighteen and nineteen, we should understand this as meaning the entire book, not just certain parts.

Because the Revelation agrees with the rest of the Bible, we can also say that the *Book of Mormon* is an addition to the Bible, which would fall under this curse. The New Testament agrees with, and does not contradict, the Revelation chapter one passage discussed above, whereas the *Book of Mormon* does not agree. This is devastating to the Mormon faith because it was written by a man who will (or has), because of his actions, apparently receive(d) curses from God according to Revelation chapter twenty-two, and because it directly contradicts what the Bible teaches. It is not the Bible that is corrupted, but the fruit that Smith produced tells us that it is Joseph Smith.

Everyone knows that if the foundation is destroyed, then the whole structure falls. But the problem is that the Bible is definitely not corrupted, and we have strong evidence that it is not. Critics will often say that the Bible was corrupted and will use the analogy of the children's game of telephone, which begins with a group of kids who whisper one sentence that is to be whispered exactly as heard from one child to the next. But,

---

[137] Joseph Smith, *Book of Mormon*, 2 Nephi 25:23.

[138] By the time Revelation chapter one was written, the gospel was established in the world.

by the end of the game, the one sentence is nothing like what the first kid heard. The problem with this is that when the gospel writers (for instance) finished their writing, they would give it away to the person to whom they were writing. Then it would be copied by a scribe, and the writer would get it back, and then it would be given away to be copied again and again. Then the copies of the copies would be copied, and it spread like wildfire. The likely reason we do not have the original autographs is because they were passed around so much that they literally dissolved in people's hands. We know that today there are numerous New Testament manuscripts in the original language (*Koine*) from as early as the second century, and if we count the manuscripts collected that were translated into another language, such as Syriac or Latin, there are considerably more ancient manuscripts and fragments.

In order for biblical corruption to happen, all of these handwritten manuscripts would have to be brought back and burned in a pile and rewritten. Needless to say, this would be impossible. One can literally compare these manuscripts from two thousand years ago and see that any variants or spelling errors by the scribes who copied them do not amount to any doctrinal or covenantal changes whatsoever. This topic will be more deeply explored in chapter six.

Second Timothy chapter three says, "All scripture is given by inspiration of God, and is profitable for doctrine, for reproof, for correction, for instruction in righteousness: That the man of God may be perfect, thoroughly furnished unto all good works."[139] This is true yesterday, today, and will be for eternity.

They Both Present Challenges to the Reader of Their Supposed Sacred Books

The gauntlet is thrown at your feet by both of these false religions, and more specifically, from both founders. The Quran says, "And if

---

[139] 2 Ti. 3:16–17.

you are in doubt as to that which we have revealed to our servant, then produce a chapter like it and call on your witnesses besides Allah if you are truthful."[140] What is going on here is that the reader is challenged to create something "*as beautiful*" as the Quran, because the author of the Quran believes it to be impossible. In any case, this does not attest to the truth of the Quran. For instance, I may personally not be able to write anything like the Lord of the Rings, or an epic poem by T. S. Eliot, yet it is true that someone clearly could.

Speaking of such, there is a similar argument for Mormonism, which is that no one could possibly write something with all of those cities and details of what went on that are in the *Book of Mormon*, but again, I appeal to the Lord of the Rings. J. R. R. Tolkien not only gave every character a name and a story, but also developed worlds, and even a language(!). This was all performed in the name of fiction.

Similar to the Quran, Joseph Smith presents a challenge to his readers in the *Book of Mormon*:

> And when ye shall receive these things, I would exhort you that ye would ask God, the Eternal Father, in the name of Christ, if these things [in the *Book of Mormon*] are not true; and if ye shall ask with a sincere heart, with real intent, having faith in Christ, he will manifest the truth of it unto you, by the power of the Holy Ghost. And by the power of the Holy Ghost ye may know the truth of all things.[141]

What about those who read the Quran under this principle? Is something true just because I believe it in my heart? Jeremiah chapter seventeen says that "The heart is deceitful above all things, and desperately

---

[140]M. H. Shakir, ed., *The Quran*, Sura 2:23.

[141]Joseph Smith, *Book of Mormon*. Moroni 10:4–5.

wicked: who can know it?"[142] In other words, do not think only with your heart! One's feelings should not determine the truth on such matters.

There Is a Major Focus from Both on Endless, Blissful Sex at Death

It is interesting that both religions are very *man-centered* as alluded to above. Not woman-and-man-centered, or just woman, but specifically man-centered. How can we tell? Because at death, there are endless rewards of sex. Muslim men will supposedly get seventy-two perpetual virgins, and Mormon men will gain endless celestial sex in order to populate their own planet. Note what the Quran states: "Thus (shall it be), and we will wed them with Houris [a beautiful, young virgin companion of a faithful Muslim in heaven] pure, beautiful ones."[143] Also, "Surely for those who guard (against evil) is achievement, Gardens and vineyards, And voluptuous women of equal age; And a pure cup."[144] These are not the only places one can find a discussion concerning the rewards in heaven for a Muslim, but the point is made.

In Mormonism, we find the following:

> The Savior was begotten by the Father of His spirit, by the same Being who is the Father of our spirits, and that is all the organic difference between Jesus Christ and you and me. And a difference there is between our Father and us consists in that He has gained His Exaltation, and has obtained eternal lives. The principle of eternal lives is an eternal existence, eternal duration, eternal Exaltation. Endless are His kingdoms, endless His thrones and His dominions, and endless are His

---

[142]Jer. 17:9.

[143]M. H. Shakir, ed., *The Quran*, Sura 44:54.

[144]Ibid. Sura 78:31–34

posterity; they never will cease to multiply from this time henceforth and forever.[145]

What is scary here is not only the doctrines about the endless celestial sex, but also the number of differences in theology between Christians and Mormons. It is a curious thing why Mormons want to be labeled just another Christian denomination. The above quote from Joseph Smith should clue us in as to why Mormons who adhere to this will never be considered Christians by Christians. They do not follow the real Jesus. Not only that, but the Mormon Jesus had a beginning, where the Biblical Jesus did not;[146] the Mormon Heavenly Father was once a regular man as the above citation alludes (as many other passages in Mormon material); the biblical God the Father never had a beginning.[147]

The Mormon logic looks like this: from the above citation, we find that the Mormon Jesus was begotten by Heavenly Father. This Mormon Heavenly Father is also the father of our spirits (implying the existence of "Heavenly Mother"). Heavenly Father (a being of *flesh and bones*, as discussed in chapter two) has gained his Exaltation, and because of such, he is the producer of spirit children (through sexual reproduction). Elsewhere, according to Joseph Smith, we can also have the same Exaltation that Heavenly Father has.[148] Marriage is a requirement for this Exaltation. This implies that Heavenly Father had a beginning, and also that there are multiple "gods."

Up to this point, we have several similarities between Mormonism and Islam. Does it make them the same religion? Definitely not. Does it make them connected? I believe so. This list is far from exhaustive. There are many other similarities not mentioned. These comparisons

---

[145]Brigham Young. *Journal of Discourses volume 4* (Liverpool: S. W. Richards, 1857), 218. Public Domain. https://contentdm.lib.byu.edu/digital/collection/JournalOfDiscourses3/id/541.

[146]See Jn. 1:1.

[147]See Isa. 44:8.

[148]See *Doctrine and Covenants* 132:19–38.

are enough to see the same tracks in the snow, and also see the "personality" of the demon behind all of this deception.

Motivations of Joseph Smith

Heavenly Father resides in a suspicious existence, is suspicious himself, and his prophet is suspicious. With all of this in mind, we can now conclude that Joseph Smith, even though he was very well versed in the Bible and even in theology in some respects, changed the doctrines and truth claims because he was after something that benefitted himself. Cold-case detective J. Warner Wallace explains in his book, *Cold Case Christianity*, that there are only three basic things that motivate criminals to act in criminal manner. Basically, it boils down to money, sex, and power.[149] How does Joseph Smith measure up against this? He received fifty dollars from Martin Harris according to the History of Joseph Smith which equates in 2020 to well over a thousand dollars. But that was just the beginning. In *Doctrine and Covenants*, one reads,

> And this shall be the beginning of the tithing of my people. And after that, those who have thus been tithed shall pay one-tenth of all their interest annually; and this shall be a standing law unto them forever, for my holy priesthood, saith the Lord. Verily I say unto you, it shall come to pass that all those who gather unto the land of Zion shall be tithed of their surplus properties, and shall observe this law, *or they shall not be found worthy to abide among you.* And I say unto you, *if my people observe not this law*, to keep it holy, and by this law sanctify the land of Zion unto me, that my statutes and my judgments may be kept thereon, that it may be

---

[149]J. Warner Wallace. *Cold-Case Christianity: A homicide detective investigates the claims of the gospels* (Colorado Springs: David C. Cook, 2013), 240.

most holy, behold, verily I say unto you, *it shall not be a land of Zion unto you.*[150]

In other words, it is the law to tithe 10 percent of annual income, and one is an outcast if he does not tithe. Seeing what the Mormon "Church" is today, I think one can see that money was a motivator in the beginning and is still. Smith's motivation for sex and power have already been demonstrated in this chapter as well. In any event, Joseph Smith manipulated people through mangling the Bible, because he saw how it could grab a hold of people's hearts. He knew that people already had presuppositions about the Word of God, so he used it and changed it in a manner that benefitted him. His plagiarism of the biblical text was necessary because his own words would not have any authority himself. This he most assuredly came to understand through trial and error. So, what he does is claim that an authority outside of himself (much like Islam) is what revealed all this material to him.

Summary

Mormons really do believe that men can potentially become gods someday, if all the qualifications are met according to their scriptures. Not only does this idea raise some blazing red flags, but the sources from which this idea came are highly questionable and downright suspicious because of other behaviors and beliefs from such as well. It seems that certain patterns can be detected in order to reveal true motivations, and because of such, not only the idea that men can potentially become gods needs a closer look, but so does the one source from which all of this came: Joseph Smith.

---

[150]Joseph Smith, *Doctrine and Covenants*, section 119:3–6; emphasis added.

Chapter Four:

Biblical and Philosophical Arguments Against the Doctrine of Exaltation

"Then said Jesus ... If ye continue in my word, then are ye my disciples indeed; And ye shall know the truth, and the truth shall make you free." ~ John 8:31–32

IN CHAPTER TWO, there was a brief discussion regarding how the beginning of the doctrine of exaltation plays out in the beginning of a Mormon's life, as in the beginning of the path of the Exaltation process. A Mormon man begins life as a human from an earthly perspective, but then becomes a god if given enough time and if he lived a righteous life from the Mormon perspective. In contrast to Christianity, the idea is not only idolatry in its purest form but is also offensive in the eyes of a biblical Christian, simply because of how the Bible regards human beings and our sin nature. In Romans chapter three, verses ten through eighteen (remember that the Bible is one of Mormonism's sacred texts), we have a powerful description of what the human condition is like before one has a personal relationship with the one true God:

As it is written, there is none righteous, no, not one: There is none that understandeth, there is none that seeketh after God. They are all gone out of the way, they are together become unprofitable; there is none that doeth good, no, not one. Their throat is an open sepulchre; with their tongues they have used deceit; the poison of asps is under their lips: Whose mouth is full of cursing and bitterness: Their feet are swift to shed blood: Destruction and misery are in their ways: And the way of peace have they not known: There is no fear of God before their eyes.[151]

There is a vast difference between the way a Mormon views human nature and the way a Christian views human nature. Also, briefly discussed in chapter three, Lynn Wilder, a Christian who was a former Mormon as well as a tenured Brigham Young University professor in Utah, writes in her book, *Unveiling Grace* about her view of human nature while she was a Mormon that Jesus was essentially, "A sin janitor [who] kept sweeping my sins away."[152] This is in the sense that as one lives his life, Jesus follows along and cleans up after him; whatever that person cannot do toward earning his own salvation, Jesus picks up the slack. This goes to show what kind of mindset that a Mormon has about the nature of human beings, that people are not inherently evil, and that Jesus is just someone who cleans things up in the wake of a sinful human being plowing his way through life.

We have already discussed how Mormonism teaches who Jesus is differently than biblical Christianity and that Mormonism teaches that the Bible is corrupt regarding the content of Second Nephi chapter twenty-five, verse twenty-three: "For we labor diligently to write, to persuade our children, and also our brethren, to believe in Christ, and to be reconciled to God; for we know that it is by grace that we are saved, after all we can do."[153] Compare this again to what the Apostle Paul says in Ephesians chapter two: "For by grace are ye saved through

---

[151]Ro. 3:10–18.

[152]Lynn Wilder. *Unveiling* Grace. 213.

[153]Joseph Smith. *Book of Mormon*. 2 Nephi 25:23.

faith; and that not of yourselves: it is the gift of God: Not of works, lest any man should boast."[154] The phrase, "*not a result of works*" is in strong opposition to what the Latter-day Saints teach. A "*gift of God*" is also not something that can be earned, yet this is exactly what Mormonism teaches, that one is working his way towards salvation and Jesus cleans up the mess he leaves behind. So, in Mormonism's most primary and sacred scriptures, we find in context that Jesus, plus works, equals salvation.

The ultimate significance about this is that only one of these views concerning the reality of human nature (and destination!) from God's perspective can be correct, because they fundamentally oppose one another, but this is where the doctrine of exaltation begins, that a Mormon is inherently good, or at least not totally depraved.

Either God sees those who are not in a personal relationship with Him that they are full of sin and all such sin must be dealt with or enter into eternal damnation as the Bible teaches (which is one reason why Jesus died, to be a substitutionary atonement for our sin[155]) or, as Mormonism teaches, that Heavenly Father sees those who are not in a personal relationship with him as going to the lowest form of Mormon heaven, because there is at least some good in him, which really is not even a bad eternal experience at all. Either we earn our way to heaven (if even partially), or entrance into heaven is a free gift. Even more simply put, salvation is either a gift or it is not a gift, but payment for good works.

The Implied Mormon Reality

We have discussed many inconsistencies that regard the doctrine of exaltation and what it means for Mormonism, and now it is time to discuss what some of these teachings imply. There are several things

---

[154]Eph. 2:8–9.

[155]See Heb. 2:17–18, 4:15–16, 7:25, 9:22; Jesus is the perfect sacrifice because He is truly human. He is also truly God and because of such can forgive sins.

can be pointed out here. One of them is that if it is true about the reality of God that he was at one time in his existence a man, and had a god over himself, then this brings up a lot of questions that Mormons do not typically seem to think about or address.

As we are in the airplane from fifty-thousand feet above ground and seeing people being born, living their lives, dying, and then becoming gods, with the *principle of causality* in mind, we must question *why* this is happening. For instance, who or what is it that put into place the plan of Exaltation? This seems to be one of the greatest questions regarding the doctrine of exaltation.

What if It Is True That Men Become Gods?

Even if this Law of the gods (the doctrine of exaltation) were true, then it would seem to ultimately prove that only one God exists, simply because there must be an explanation for this law to be in existence from eternity past in the first place. Remember, every law requires a lawgiver. Every effect has a cause. The Law of the gods *is* an effect. So, who wrote the Law of the gods? Who is the cause of this pattern? The answer is that if the Law of the gods were true, then the one true and Supreme God wrote this law. The problem is that this is also absurd. If it were true, it would reduce the doctrine of exaltation in Mormonism to a person becoming something less than what the *one Supreme God* is, never being able to attain the place where God is, therefore the one Supreme God would then be greater than every other "god." Mormon scriptures teach that men can become gods, but even then, they would simply still be men, even if they had special powers or authority, because Heavenly Father is "*as we are now.*"

What this also means is that if the Law of the gods is true, then Mormonism is false. One reason for this is because if reality described by what Mormonism teaches is true, then men can become gods of their own planets. This would require the fact that there is a law written in order for all of this to take place; in order for it all to happen. So, for it to happen, this means that someone wrote such a law which transcends all of the gods (Heavenly Fathers) in the Mormon infinite universe or the Mormon infinite multiverse. Not only does the law that was written transcend all of the Mormon gods in the universe or multiverse, but so does the Supreme Being who wrote the law. This means that Mormons then, do not worship the Supreme Being, but in fact, they worship a man with the word *"God"* as a *nickname* but is not actually his title. If the reality about Heavenly Father is true (that he was once a man), then Mormonism is false, because the actual *Supreme Being* is not worshiped by Mormons, even though they say that they worship the Supreme Being as discussed in chapter three. Again, if the doctrine of exaltation is *true*, then this means that Mormonism is ultimately *false*. They are worshiping a being under the authority and power under *actual* Supreme Being (the one who made the Law), a mere man, and so they do not understand what the word *supreme* means. The actual Supreme Being is not under the authority of another being. Mormons miss the point entirely. It seems to me that the Mormon usage of the phrase, Supreme Being, is the major thing that hinders a Mormon from thinking beyond his own doctrine of exaltation. This is all immediately significant because the doctrine of exaltation is *fundamental* to Mormon theology and *soteriology* (i.e. the study of salvation) and is in the sacred and foundational scriptures in Mormonism.

So, because Mormons say that they worship the one Supreme Being, yet this being has beings in authority over him (not only *his* Heavenly Father, but also the actual Supreme Being who wrote the law), then Mormons do not worship the actual Supreme Being, and the Mormon sacred scriptures are false because they both (Mormons and their scriptures) claim that they worship the Supreme Being (which is false), and also imply that there is more than one Supreme Being (which is also false). So, if the doctrine of exaltation is true, then Mormonism is false because their scriptures are false and completely contradict themselves. Both theologically and philosophically, the Law of the gods fails under its own weight.

Reductio ad Absurdum

One of the major motivations for this book as mentioned in chapter one, is because Mormons are claiming to know the truth about the reality of God. If men become gods when they die, then according to what is required of Mormon cosmology in order for this to logically work, it would have to be the case that there are an infinite number of worlds, and infinite number of planets, and an infinite number of people. Heavenly Father is, as discovered throughout this book, an exalted man. "As man now is, *God once was*...." So, we must peer into the logic of the situation of this exalted man who came from another planet. Say that the name of Heavenly Father was Harold[156] on the planet that he lived on. Harold must have had parents, and according to *Doctrine and Covenants* mentioned multiple times, Harold *must* be married. So, Harold had a wife on his planet. This couple who are now apparently elevated to the status of gods, must have had parents on the planet that they inhabited.

Not only this, but who was Harold's and his wife's god? Who populated the world in which Harold lived? Let's say his name was Frank. So, Frank lived on a different planet than Harold, and Frank became an exalted man and created worlds for people to live on and Harold was one of those people. Harold worshiped Frank, though he would never call him that. He would endearingly refer to him as "*Heavenly Father*." Similarly, the Mormons on planet earth would never call their Heavenly Father by his worldly name. So, the pattern continues. Frank had a god who was a man named Ralph. Ralph had a god who once was a man and his name was Clarence, etc., etc., *ad infinitum*.

Mormonism unquestionably boils down to people worshiping other exalted people. Honestly, what is the real difference if one worships another now, as opposed to in the next life? If a man is *becoming* Heavenly Father while on earth, then why would he be any better after

---

[156]Actually, most Mormons would likely say that his name was *Elohim*.

he dies? For the simple fact of time? Simply because that man will never be the god of an equal man from the same world. It only seems to work with following generations, so to speak, from one world to the next.

William Lane Craig explains that the Muslim philosopher Abū Ḥāmid Muḥammad ibn Muḥammad al-Ghazālī believed that we cannot really have an actual infinite number of anything (let alone, gods). In other words, "Ghazālī had no problem with the existence of merely *potential* infinites, for these are just ideal limits. But when we come to an *actual* infinite, we're dealing with a collection that is not growing toward infinity as a limit but is already complete."[157] What this means is that an unlimited number of gods is impossible because in Mormonism, people continue to become gods all the time. If they are adding to the number of infinite gods, then the number cannot be infinite in the first place.

The implied and actual claims of the *Doctrine and Covenants* all makes the principle of causality no less of a requirement. We know that everything that begins to exist has a cause for its existence. Mormons generally say that there is no beginning to the universe. This belief is required in order for their entire religion to logically follow. Or they would argue that the infinite multiverse exists, but even if the multiverse did exist, there would still have to be something that metaphysically causes the generation of these multiple universes to come into existence. In other words, the principle of causality still applies to the multiverse. So, it still holds that everything that begins to exist has a cause. We can know this to be true simply through the evidence that we observe both presently and historically, and experiences that we have. At this point, we should discuss the Kalam Cosmological Argument because it will help with understanding something both now and later:

1. Whatever begins to exist has a cause.

---

[157]William Lane Craig, *On Guard: Defending your faith with reason and precision* (Colorado Springs: David C. Cook, 2010), 79; emphasis added.

2. The universe began to exist.
3. Therefore, the universe has a cause.[158]

Since the universe had a beginning, then it is only possible that a finite number of planets exists. Again, the same rules apply to the multiverse. There can only be a finite number of universes in the multiverse because it is also not a complete set. Length of time does not take away the necessity for causation. A universe in the multiverse cannot be added to an infinite set of universes.

Craig continues to reduce the argument for a physical, infinite past to absurdity:

> "Second ... Suppose Jupiter completes an orbit once every 12 years and Saturn once every 30 years and the sphere of the stars once every 36,000 years. If the universe is eternal and these planets have been orbiting from eternity, then each of these [cosmological] bodies has completed an infinite number of orbits, and yet one will have completed twice as many or thousands of times as many orbits as another, which is absurd."[159]

Because planets, even in our own solar system, revolve around the sun at different amounts of time, then how can an actual infinite be possible? How could one planet revolve twice as much as another planet and yet both of them revolved around the sun an infinite number of times? The answer is that this is impossible.

Not only does a physical, actual, infinite past not exist philosophically, but it also cannot exist scientifically speaking. The Second Law of Thermodynamics shows us that if the universe were eternal, it would

---

[158] William Lane Craig, *Reasonable Faith: Christian truth and apologetics* (Wheaton, IL: Crossway, 2008), 111.

[159] Ibid. 96–97.

have run out of energy by now.[160] If there is a finite amount of energy (which we know that there is because we can observe not only old cars rotting away in fields, but we can also observe that stars eventually burn out), in an infinite amount of time, then we would have run out of energy an infinite number of years ago. But this is absurd because we still observe and experience energy.

What if It Is Not True that Men Become Gods?

Then Mormonism is still false (at least as far as the doctrine of exaltation is concerned). If the Law of the gods is not true, then Mormonism is false because becoming a god is what the hope of Mormonism is based on. This is likely the most fundamental doctrine in Mormonism. The doctrine of exaltation is what most blatantly sets Mormons apart from Biblical Christianity (aside from other heretical beliefs that Jesus is a created being and is not God in the flesh; the belief that God has a wife, and the belief that Satan and Jesus are brothers, et al.), this being the belief that a man can become a god, and the belief that God was once a man, *as we are now.* Remember the Lorenzo Snow Couplet: "As man is, god once was; as god is, man may become." So then if the Law of the gods is not true, then Mormonism is false. This is what the Mormon sacred scripture, *Doctrine and Covenants,* teaches, which is the doctrine of exaltation. Again, what this means is that if the doctrine of exaltation is true, then Mormonism is false (because they do not worship the one true God). But if the doctrine of exaltation is false, then Mormonism is false (because this doctrine is fundamental and foundational to Mormonism). Either way, then, whether the Law of the gods is true or false, it means that Mormonism is ultimately false.

Therefore, the ultimate cause of the pattern that men become "gods" in Mormonism, if true, proves that there is only one true Supreme God, which creates a number of logical, philosophical, and theological

---

[160]Ibid. 141.

inconsistencies in Mormon doctrine as one can see, but also the ultimate cause of this pattern that men become "gods" transcends those who become "gods" themselves, which really makes one wonder how much of a "God" a person can really become if there are other beings that transcend him. This all goes to show what a low view Mormons really have about Heavenly Father. It amounts to idolatry in its purest form, biblically speaking. It is an *in-your-face* violation of the First of the Ten Commandments.

The doctrine of exaltation is the hope that Mormonism is built upon. The hope of Mormonism is found wanting if the doctrine of exaltation is not true. If one were to ask if the doctrine of exaltation is an *essential* belief to Mormonism, a Mormon would have to say that it is. For one thing, this doctrine of exaltation is how Mormonism describes eternal life as we have seen above.[161] This is how Mormonism answers the fundamental question of life, "What happens after we die?"

To reiterate and summarize then, the reason Mormonism is false if the doctrine of exaltation is *true* is because Mormons are not worshiping the one Supreme Being. This is proven by the Law of the gods. They are worshiping a being under the *actual* Supreme Being (the one who made the Law), a mere man, and they do not understand what the word *supreme* means. The reason Mormonism is false if the doctrine of exaltation is *false* is because this is what their scriptures fundamentally teach and is the ultimate hope of a Mormon.

The Law of the Gods Is Ultimately an Argument for the Existence of the One Supreme God

Not only does the Law of the gods show that Mormonism is false whether or not it is true or false, but in a real sense, it can be used as an argument for the existence of the one Supreme God. The Supreme Being, by definition, is the most powerful being who holds the highest

---

[161]Church of Jesus Christ of the Latter-day Saints. *Gospel Principles.*

authority in all existence. Mormons call Heavenly Father the Supreme Being, and biblical Christians know God as the Supreme Being. But the same fundamental law of non-contradiction applies here in both claims as well. But the thing is, if Heavenly Father has a god that is over him, then that being is the Supreme Being. But if the Heavenly Grandfather, so to speak, has a god over him, then that being is the Supreme Being. The problem with this is that it can go backwards in time for eternity … Heavenly Great-Grandfather to Heavenly Great-Great-Grandfather and so on. *This idea is only considering one lineage!* So, then the Supreme Being must be the being who got all of this started. After all, the Law of the gods must begin somewhere. This is simply in accord with the *principle of causality*.

In order to fully grasp this, let's look back to the Kalam Cosmological Argument for the existence of God developed by William Lane Craig:

1. Everything that begins to exist has a cause for its existence.
2. The universe began to exist.
3. Therefore, the universe has a cause.[162]

This is a typical way to understand the Kalam Cosmological Argument, as also Norman Geisler even explains it in a similar, concise manner as well:

1. The universe had a beginning.
2. Anything that had a beginning must have been caused by something else.
3. Therefore, the universe was caused by something else, which we call, "God."[163]

---

[162]William Lane Craig, *Reasonable Faith*, 96.

[163]Norman L. Geisler and Ronald M. Brooks. *When Skeptics Ask: A handbook on Christian evidences.* (Grand Rapids: Baker Books, 2013), 10.

Now that we have had a small metaphysical look at cosmological arguments, we can see that the conclusions to these syllogisms are essentially the same. They both point to the Greatest Conceivable Being, which is God. They also are based on the simple yet powerful principle of causality. This is the main reason to bring these to the reader's attention, in order that the principle of causality might be more deeply considered.

Now, observe the following collection of syllogisms from the Mormon perspective, keeping the principle of causality in mind:

1. If I can become a god when I die, then it is safe to assume that others can as well.
2. I can become a god when I die.
3. Therefore, I can conclude that there are numerous gods from earth.

———————

1. If Heavenly Father came from another planet in the universe, then I can assume that where he came from also had other people becoming gods.
2. Heavenly Father came from another planet.
3. Therefore, I can conclude that there are numerous gods in the universe.

The two syllogisms above just go to show the inevitable vast number of gods that would logically exist. Remember, that in Mormon scripture, there is nowhere found an explanation of *why* this is happening, or what started it all.

1. If there is a beginning to Mormon men becoming gods Therefore, the law that causes them to become gods transcends these gods.

2. There is a beginning to men becoming gods according to the principle of causality.
3. Therefore, the law that causes them to become gods transcends this collection of gods.

The above syllogism gives an explanation from the Mormon perspective how the prior two syllogisms with the conclusion of this one is logically consistent.

1. If there is a beginning to the universe (or multiverse), then there is one Supreme God who caused this Law of the gods to take effect.
2. There is a beginning.
3. Therefore, there is one Supreme God who caused this Law of the gods (or this pattern) to take effect.

———————•———————

1. If there is *not* a beginning to the universe (or perhaps an infinite multiverse exists), the only way to account for the pattern of men becoming gods is by a law put into effect by a Supreme God since it transcends all Mormon Heavenly Fathers, or that there are no Mormon gods at all.
2. There is not a beginning (again this is from a Mormon perspective).
3. Therefore, the only way to account for the system or pattern of men becoming gods is by a law put into effect by the Supreme God since it transcends the collection of Heavenly Fathers, or there are no Mormon gods at all.

The above two arguments conclude through the principle of causality that whether or not there is a beginning to the universe, there must be a cause for the Law of the gods.

Together, these syllogisms (which may not all be completely necessary) bring us to…

The Mormon Cosmological Argument (MCA) for the Existence of One Supreme God[164]

1. If the Law of the gods transcends the gods (Heavenly Fathers) in Mormonism, then there is one Supreme God who wrote the Law or caused its existence.
2. The Law of the gods transcends all Heavenly Fathers.
3. Therefore, there is one Supreme God, who is the author of the Law.

What this means is that from the Mormon perspective, there ultimately must be one Supreme God, but Mormons do not worship Him. What it also means is that this collection of Heavenly Fathers is essentially an argument for the existence of the one Supreme God, namely, the God of the Bible. The reason this is the case is because of the implied philosophical *set* of Heavenly Fathers or the plurality of gods in Mormonism exist, and with the principle of causality in mind, there must be a Supreme God who caused the set to exist. Ultimately, then, Mormonism is impossible.

The Forge of the Great Blacksmith

It seems that the following illustration can be of further help in understanding not only the metaphysics of the Mormon doctrine of exaltation, but also why it fails. Imagine a blacksmith, working in his shop, and he is hammering away at the red-hot iron that is before him. The sparks are flying as he smashes iron folded onto itself, seeking

---

[164]"Mormon Cosmological Argument" or "MCA" is also acceptable.

to shape his object into something meaningful. The reason for all of this activity is that he is a blacksmith. Blacksmithing is what he does. Similarly with a gunsmith. The gunsmith builds guns and fixes them because guns are his subject. He takes parts and machines them to fit other parts and puts them together. He is an expert at doing what he does. He fashions guns. The same is true for a goldsmith, a silversmith, and even a locksmith. Their products are effects, and all their effects have causes.

The thing about the Law of the gods is that there must be a God-smith; *the Great Blacksmith*, so to speak, hammering out gods with the coals burning and the sparks flying and the water steaming. It is not as if the plurality of gods in Mormonism are making gods themselves, or have always existed, but they are literally all just the result of being made a god. But since this ancestry of gods can be traced back (in Mormon thinking) for an infinite regress of time, there had to have been something that began it all, otherwise it reaches to the absurd. This Beginner must be the Great Blacksmith (or the God-smith). The forge of the gods must be operated by the Great Blacksmith (i.e. the Supreme Being). The problem is, Mormonism has no answer as to who this Great Blacksmith is, or where he comes from, much like the law of Karma, as discussed in chapter two. The ultimate question is indeed, "*Why?*" as in, *why* do men become gods, and because there is no answer for such a question Mormons are blindly believing in and trusting in such a doctrine.

Mormon Objections to the Impossibility of Men Becoming a God

I have heard John chapter ten, verses thirty-four through thirty-nine, and Psalm chapter eighty-two, verse six being used to support the idea that *men can become "gods"* in Mormonism since I learned about the existence of Mormonism. Refuting this is much easier than one might think.

Let's look first at the context of John chapter ten, verses thirty through thirty-nine:

> "I and my Father are one." Then the Jews took up stones again to stone him. Jesus answered them, "Many good works have I shewed you from my Father; for which of those works do ye stone me?" The Jews answered him, saying, "For a good work we stone thee not; but for blasphemy; and because that thou, being a man, makest thyself God." Jesus answered them, "Is it not written in your law, 'I said, Ye are gods?' If he called them gods, unto whom the word of God came, and the scripture cannot be broken; Say ye of him, whom the Father hath sanctified, and sent into the world, Thou blasphemest; because I said, I am the Son of God? If I do not the works of my Father, believe me not. But if I do, though ye believe not me, believe the works: that ye may know, and believe, that the Father is in me, and I in him."
>
> Therefore they sought again to take him: but he escaped out of their hand.[165]

The Jews wanted to kill Jesus not because of His miracles, but because of His *words*. Look at verses thirty-two and thirty-three in the above passage again: "Jesus answered them, 'Many good works have I shewed you from my Father; for which of those works do ye stone me?' The Jews answered him, saying, 'For a good work we stone thee not; but for blasphemy; and because that thou, being a man, makest thyself God.'"[166] Jesus, on the other hand, kept pointing to His *works* (i.e. *miracles*). "For which of these do you stone me?" Finally, He

---

[165]Jn. 10:30–39; emphasis added.

[166]Jn. 10:32–33.

meets them where they are at and beats them at their own game. The logic of Jesus in verses thirty-five and thirty-six looks like this:

1. Men, to whom the Word of God *came*, were called *"gods"* (meaning *judges*; more below).
2. Jesus was *sent* by God (as the *Living Word* of God).
3. How much more realistic is it then, to call Jesus (the one sent by God to men), "God?!"

Men, who *received* the Word of God, were unable to do anything except make judgments. *Jesus*, on the other hand (*the sent, living Word of God*) is able to perform miracles. Yet *men* are called "gods." Jesus is claiming that He is God and is also proving it by the miracles he performs. He says in verse thirty-seven, "If I am not doing the works of my Father, then do not believe me."

Jesus is referring to Psalm chapter eighty-two in this conversation with the Jews in John chapter ten. It is important to note here that the word in Hebrew for the word "God" can also be translated as the word "judge."[167] That said, if Psalm chapter eighty-two were a stage play or theatrical work, it would look like this:

[**Narrator**:] God standeth in the congregation of the mighty;
    he judgeth among the gods.
[**God**:] How long will ye judge unjustly,
    and accept the persons of the wicked? Selah.
Defend the poor and fatherless:
    do justice to the afflicted and needy.
Deliver the poor and needy:
    rid them out of the hand of the wicked.
They know not, neither will they understand;
    they walk on in darkness:

---

[167]See Ex. 21:6; 22:8 in the *New International Version*.

all the foundations of the earth are out of course.

I have said, <u>Ye are gods</u>;

and all of you are <u>children of the most High</u>.

But <u>ye shall die like men</u>, and fall like one of the princes.

[**"gods"**:] Arise, O God, judge the earth:

for thou shalt inherit all nations!"[168]

It is clear from this passage that "gods" are not the same kind of being as the one referred to in the first verse. For one thing, the *gods* that God is *in the midst of,* will "die like men." Why will they die like men? Because they *are* men. Remember that this Hebrew word translated "God" can also mean "judge." Mankind are *definitely* judges. In Genesis chapter one, verse twenty-six, "And God said, 'Let us make man in our image, after our likeness: and let them have dominion over the fish of the sea, and over the fowl of the air, and over the cattle, and over all the earth, and over every creeping thing that creepeth upon the earth.'"[169] God made us *rulers* ("let them have dominion"). Does not being a ruler require making judgments? It appears to be inescapable. But, with this out of the way, we can now get to the problem of using these verses for scriptural support of men becoming "gods" in Mormonism.

When Mormons use the word "God" in the sense that this is what "man may become," they are using the word with the definition of an "all-powerful being," not as "a judge." This commits the fallacy of equivocation, which is calling two different things by the same name. It would be like saying, "Warm ice cream is better than cold ice cream. After all, nothing is better than cold ice cream, and warm ice cream is better than nothing." Do you see how this is using the word "nothing" in two totally different ways? The fallacy is in ownership versus using

---

[168]Ps. 82; emphasis added.

[169]Gen. 1:26; emphasis added.

a figure of speech. "*Nothing is better than...*" is a figure of speech but having nothing deals with not owning anything.

How about the following for another example: "Loud music is a real headache. Two aspirin will make a headache go away. Therefore, two aspirin will make loud music go away." The issue seems to be clear; the word *headache* is equal to nuisance in one sense, but then, the same word is equal to having pain in one's head in another sense.

This is the same issue with the way Mormons are using the John chapter ten passage and Psalm chapter eighty-two, verse six: "Jesus acknowledged that God (all-powerful being) called men "*gods*" (judges), therefore, I can become a God (all-powerful being)."

The thing is, when Mormons point you to John chapter ten or Psalm chapter eighty-two, verse six to argue that men become gods, just bring them to the source in Psalm chapter eighty-two, verse six, and have them read the next verse (seven): "Nevertheless, like men you shall die, and fall like any prince."

On the Trinity: The Orthodox Christian Understanding

Mormons do not believe in the Trinity.[170] They believe instead in three gods (tritheism), which seems to be more consistent with their belief of the doctrine of exaltation. One reason tritheism is more consistent for Mormons is because the Trinity is by nature, a doctrine which stands against the doctrine of exaltation. The reality of the doctrine of exaltation and the reality of the Doctrine of the Trinity cannot both be correct, simply because they contradict one another.

First, let's summarize the biblical Christian understanding of the doctrine of the Trinity. Norman Geisler says that "The Doctrine of the Trinity is based on two basic biblical teachings: 1) there is one and only one God; and 2) there are three distinct persons who are

---

[170]Some might say that they do, but when Mormons or non-Mormons say that they do or not, everyone agrees that the Mormon version of the Trinity is nothing like the biblical Christian doctrine of the Trinity.

God: The Father, the Son, and the Holy Spirit. The Trinity is the only logical conclusion from these two premises."[171] To reiterate and expand on our discussion in chapter two, we again start in the Bible at the *Shema*, which is found in Deuteronomy chapter six, verse four, "Hear, O Israel: The LORD our God is one LORD."[172] The fact is, biblical Christians are monotheistic. This verse, Deuteronomy chapter six, *is in* the Christian Bible. But the thing is, there is a lot more biblical material until we reach the end of this authoritative collection of books. This ancient collection of books and letters that we call the Bible brings us deeper into an understanding of who God is, and what He is like.

Before we move on with this discussion, it is also good for us to know that after having established biblically that *God is one* in the Christian faith, it is not the *only* way to describe Him. This is not where the Bible ceases in describing God. For instance, we can also biblically describe God as *love*. First John chapter four, verses seven and eight reveal this to us: "Beloved, let us love one another: for love is of God; and every one that loveth is born of God, and knoweth God. He that loveth not knoweth not God; for God is love."[173] We can further biblically describe God as *spirit* as Jesus does in John chapter four: "God is a Spirit: and they that worship him must worship him in spirit and in truth."[174] This is very contrary to what Mormons teach about God. The point here is to show the reader that a discussion of theology proper is a vast and involved topic. We can ascribe things such as attributes to God, but in Mormonism, they ascribe whole other *beings* to Heavenly Father. From their perspective, Heavenly Father was once a man and so I, as a man can become a Heavenly Father to others. Christians, however, do not associate another being to God,

---

[171]Norman Geisler and Ron Rhodes, *Conviction Without Compromise* (Eugene: Harvest House Publishers, 2008), 34.

[172]Dt. 6:4.

[173]1 Jn. 4:7–8.

[174]Jn. 4:24.

because as mentioned, God is one.[175] This all just goes to show where we theologically draw the line in associating or attributing things with God. In Mormonism, there is no such line.

Because of such things, it seems that a troubling area for many people in discussing the doctrine of the Trinity is logic. For instance, some Mormons wonder how three people can be one person, or how one being can be three beings, but this is not what Christians are saying. Trinitarian believers would also disagree with these statements and call them logical fallacies.

Geisler, in his massive *Systematic Theology*, explains how there are not really any analogies that translate perfectly when speaking of the Trinity, but says that:

> God is like a triangle, which is one figure yet has three different sides at the same time—there is a simultaneous threeness in the oneness. Of course, no analogy is perfect, since in every analogy there is a similarity and difference. The difference here is that "corners" are not persons. Nonetheless, they do illustrate how there can be a "threeness" and a oneness at the same time.[176]

The idea is interesting and useful how a triangle can illustrate a threeness and a oneness at the same time and remain logically consistent. This seems to be a major problem for Mormons, seeing the logic in the Trinity.

William Lane Craig, founder of Reasonable Faith, has this to say:

---

[175]This leads again to the question, where did the Law of the gods come from? One cannot say that it is a part of God like one of his attributes such as logic, because the Law of the gods existed before the Mormon God.

[176]Norman Geisler, *Systematic Theology*. (Bloomington: Bethany House Publishers, 2011), 551.

The doctrine of the Trinity is not the doctrine that three Gods are somehow one God. That would be clearly self-contradictory—to say there are three Gods, and these are one God. Neither is it the claim that there are three persons who are somehow one person. That, again, would be self-contradictory—to assert that there are three persons who are all one person. But the doctrine of the Trinity does not assert that there are three Gods that are one God or three persons that are one person, but it asserts that there is one God who is tri-personal. It is one God who is three persons, or, to put it another way, there is one God who has three centers of self-consciousness: the Father, the Son, and the Holy Spirit.[177]

So, just like an individual person is *one being* with *one center of self-consciousness*, God is *one being* with *three centers of self-consciousness*. This is not the same as "multiple personality disorder," as some might object, for several reasons. First, *multiple-personality disorder is not a real disorder*. Psychologists and Medical Doctors by the droves have come to this conclusion. For instance, Allen J Frances M.D., writes in a *Psychology Today* article: "Why does MPD [Multiple-Personality Disorder] keep making its periodic comebacks, despite not being a verifiable or clinically useful mental disorder?" My best guess is that the labeling of alters offers an appealing and dramatic metaphor, an idiom of distress."[178] When trying to say that Christians are saying that God has a multiple-personality disorder, it would be like saying

---

[177]William Lane Craig, "Doctrine of the Trinity (part 1)." Reasonable Faith, June 27, 2011. https://www.reasonablefaith.org/podcasts/defenders-podcast-series-2/s2-doctrine-of-god-trinity/doctrine-of-the-trinity-part-1.

[178]Allen J Frances, M.D. "*Multiple Personality: Mental Disorder, Myth, or Metaphor? Why multiple personality disorder fads come and go.*" Psychology Today, Jan 30, 2014. https://www.psychologytoday.com/us/blog/saving-normal/201401/multiple-personality-mental-disorder-myth-or-metaphor.

that He has a superhero complex, or something to that nature. The issue here is that it is a (*multiple*) categorical error because God is not a mere human, and second, because human beings cannot even have a multiple-personality disorder.

God is one being with three centers of self-consciousness. He is three in persons and one in essence. The Bible teaches this. For instance, we discussed the *Shema*, showing that in the Bible, there is only one God, but one can also see, biblically speaking, that God exists in three persons. Let's look again at John chapter ten, verses thirty through thirty-three. Jesus replies, "'I and my Father are one.' Then the Jews took up stones again to stone him. Jesus answered them, 'Many good works have I shewed you from my Father; for which of those works do ye stone me?' The Jews answered him, saying, 'For a good work we stone thee not; but for blasphemy; and because that thou, being a man, makest thyself God.'"[179]

The Jews at this time recognized the fact that if Jesus were not who He said He was, this would indeed be blasphemy. The problem is that they were blind to see the truth of who He was through His miracles.[180] The point is that the Jews picked up stones to stone Him because He was calling Himself *God*. The Jews clearly recognized this, which is why they wanted to stone Him for blasphemy. The question is, why would someone not recognize today that Jesus called Himself God? Perhaps it is because of spiritual blindness in our day as well.

Since most Christians reading this likely assume already that the Father is God, and many places in the Bible discuss the Father as God,[181] one will see here that Jesus is God, and that the Holy Spirit is God. The whole idea here is to show through the *Shema* (and other verses like it), that yes, there is one God, and through these other verses, one can see that He exists in three persons.

---

[179]Jn. 10:30–33.

[180]See Jn. 10:38.

[181]See Jn. 1:1; Mk. 1; Jn. 17 (where Jesus prays to the Father, not to Himself); Heb. 1 (where God the Father calls God the Son, "*God*" et al).

Continuing our track that *Jesus is God* from the Bible, we could look at a number of other verses, but since we just discussed one, we will observe another one before moving on.

In chapter one in the book of Revelation, verse eight reads, "'I am Alpha and Omega, the beginning and the ending,' saith the Lord, 'which is, and which was, and which is to come, the Almighty.'"[182] If a person were to ask exactly *who* the "*Alpha and the Omega*" is referring to, again, likely a Mormon might say that it is referring to *Heavenly Father*, from the phrase, "the Almighty."

Further along in the same chapter, one would find John writing this: "And when I saw him, I fell at his feet as dead. And he laid his right hand upon me, saying unto me, 'Fear not; I am the first and the last: I am he that liveth, and was dead; and, behold, I am alive for evermore, Amen; and have the keys of hell and of death.'"[183] The "*first and the last*" here is a reference to the Alpha and the Omega, which is the first letter and the last letter of the Greek alphabet. In other words, Jesus is saying here that He is God. We could also have a large discussion on what is one of the most blatant passages in scripture that reveal the deity of Jesus, which is John chapter one, verses one through three and verse fourteen, but because we have already discussed this in length in chapter two, we will now move to the person of the Holy Spirit.

In the book of Acts, chapter five, verses one through six, Luke records what took place:

> But a certain man named Ananias, with Sapphira his wife, sold a possession, And kept back part of the price, his wife also being privy to it, and brought a certain part, and laid it at the apostles' feet. But Peter said, "Ananias, why hath Satan filled thine heart to *lie to the Holy Ghost*, and to keep back part of the price of the land? Whiles

---

[182]Rev. 1:8; emphasis added.

[183]Rev. 1:17–18; emphasis added.

it remained, was it not thine own? and after it was sold, was it not in thine own power? why hast thou conceived this thing in thine heart? *thou hast not lied unto men, but unto God.*" And Ananias hearing these words fell down, and gave up the ghost: and great fear came on all them that heard these things. And the young men arose, wound him up, and carried him out, and buried him.[184]

In this passage, Peter, who is not only an early Christian, but also an Apostle of Christ, calls the Holy Spirit "God." Why would some people not want to call God what the early church calls God? Why would people not want to describe God the way the Early Church does? Perhaps it is because those who do not want to acknowledge the Trinity are so far removed from the early church that it is an extreme distinction from the early church.

Another passage worthy of discussion here is found in chapter one in the Gospel of Mark. The Trinity is in full view here just as it is in the Great Commission: "And it came to pass in those days, that Jesus came from Nazareth of Galilee, and was baptized of John in Jordan. And straightway coming up out of the water, he saw the heavens opened, and the Spirit like a dove descending upon him: And there came a voice from heaven, saying, 'Thou art my beloved Son, in whom I am well pleased.'"[185] From this, one can clearly see what was going through the mind of the ancient writer. The word, *Trinity,* was not yet invented, but the truth of the Trinity is clearly eternal. Similarly, the word, *calculus,* was not yet invented, and although calculus is often described as being *invented* by Leibniz or Newton, the fact is that it was not invented, but *discovered.*[186]

---

[184]Ac. 5:1–6; emphasis added.

[185]Mk. 1:9–11; emphasis added.

[186]Truth is never invented, but *only* discovered.

<u>Summary</u>

We have discussed many things up to this point, regarding the truth of Mormonism, that it is impossible that men can become gods, the Supreme Being, and that even from the Mormon perspective, if it is possible, then Mormonism is false. Below again is the **Mormon Cosmological Argument for the existence of the One Supreme God**:

1. If the Law of the gods transcends these Heavenly Fathers in Mormonism, then there is one Supreme God who wrote the Law or caused its existence.
2. The Law of the gods transcends all Heavenly Fathers.
3. Therefore, there is one supreme God, who is the author of the Law.

This syllogism's premises are based on the beliefs and scriptures of Mormons, resulting in a catastrophic conclusion for Mormons, but it is just another of many arguments for God's existence for Christians. The Trinity is not what Mormons believe, and because the Bible, which is one of their own sacred texts, teaches what it really is, dismantles the Mormon understanding of three gods, or tritheism, simply based on the idea of separation. If there is more than one "greatest conceivable being" or "Supreme Being," then how could they be distinguished from one to the next?

Chapter Five:

The Devastating Archaeological Assertions

"Alexamenos worships his God." ~ Ancient Roman Graffito

CONCERNS FOCUS ON issues involving the historicity of the *Book of Mormon*. Is the *Book of Mormon* really credible historically and archaeologically speaking? What does it mean for the *Doctrine and Covenants* if the *Book of Mormon* is found to be not historically and archaeologically reliable? How does it compare to the Bible? Since archaeological discoveries consist of evidence from historical events, then there should be large amounts of artifacts and ruins that still exist where the *Book of Mormon* claims that life, wars, and other major activities took place. If the *Book of Mormon* is "the most correct book of any that is on earth" but is found to be false, what does this say about everything else written or "translated" by Joseph Smith, including the *Doctrine and Covenants*, which is where one finds the heaviest teaching of the doctrine of exaltation?

Archaeology is used in apologetics because it confirms beliefs about historical events, customs, cultures, traditions, and activities to list a few benefits, but on the other hand, it can challenge historical claims through evidence. Think about it … where there was a group of Native Americans centuries ago knapping away at flint or obsidian to make arrowheads and such, and because stone does not decompose as fast as modern craft and building materials do, if we dig carefully enough, we should be able to find this residual waste of stone chips.

If someone were to claim that "primitive Native Americans never existed," the artifacts and evidence that have been found suggest that we should simply disagree with such a claim. Likewise, if there are legends and records of past events, archaeological investigation could at least indirectly confirm or deny some of these events. Whether archeology proves biblical history or puts the historicity of the *Book of Mormon* into serious question, the goal of archaeology is to learn the facts of what happened, where it happened, why it happened, who was involved, and when the actual events took place.

Biblical Archaeology Brings the Bible from Black and White to Color

There are many references that can be found in Scripture speaking of certain things such as the name of the City of David, which is found in several biblical books including Second Samuel, First and Second Kings, and First Chronicles. In other words, these places with names such as this have been in existence since early biblical times, and still exist in the present day. As opposed to other "ancient" writings such as what is found in the *Book of Mormon*, the Bible speaks of recognizable, tangible places, helping to bring the Bible to life to modern readers. The *Book of Mormon* speaks of wars, cities, and towns where the names of such are nowhere on earth to be found, but where certain events have taken place in the Bible, people have named towns and cities after these events which are still named for such.

The discoveries of the Dead Sea Scrolls in the caves at Qumran are also a strong argument in favor of biblical history. "In a cave in the Judean Desert cliffs south of Qumran, Bedouins in 1947 found the first Dead Sea scrolls. Following this discovery, Qumran was excavated by the Dominican Father R. de Vaux in the years 1951-56. A complex of buildings, extending over an area of 100 x 80 m. was uncovered, dating to the Second Temple period."[187] These scrolls were (and

---

[187]Jewish Virtual Library. *Archaeology in Israel: Qumran.* (American-Israeli Cooperative Enterprise, 2022). https://www.jewishvirtuallibrary.org/qumran.

still are) big news, and everyone was able to read about them as they were not covered up and esoteric, unlike anything that the Mormons claim about things such as with the notorious *golden plates*. As is well known, the Second Temple period ended around the year 70 AD. Since these ancient Qumran buildings had copies of the Bible (books such as Genesis, Isaiah, Psalms, and Deuteronomy), one can conclude that the highly skilled people in charge of this ancient library considered the contents of these scrolls that are saturated with history to be sacred.

The *Book of Mormon* makes some extraordinary claims about there being wars with large numbers of warriors in the Americas. The problem with this is that there has been no archaeological evidence to support these claims that the *Book of Mormon* makes. The following is part of a statement issued by the Smithsonian Institution in the eighties to some who were curious about the *Book of Mormon* being a guide for archaeologists and anthropologists to so called ancient sites found in the *Book of Mormon*.

> The Smithsonian Institution has never used the *Book of Mormon* in any way as a scientific guide. Smithsonian archeologists see no direct connection between the archeology of the New World and the subject matter of the book....
>
> Iron, steel, glass, and silk were not used in the New World before 1492 (except for occasional use of unsmelted meteoric iron). Native copper was worked used (sic) in various locations in pre-Columbian times, but true metallurgy was limited to southern Mexico and the Andean region, where its occurrence in late prehistoric times involved gold, silver, copper, and their alloys, but not iron.
>
> No reputable Egyptologist or other specialist on Old World archeology, and no expert on New World prehistory, has discovered or confirmed any

relationship between archeological remains in Mexico and archeological remains in Egypt....

Reports of findings of ancient Egyptian, Hebrew, and other Old World writings in the New World in pre-Columbian contexts have frequently appeared in newspapers, magazines, and sensational books. None of these claims has stood up to examination by reputable scholars. No inscriptions using Old World forms of writing have been shown to have occurred in any part of the Americas before 1492 except for a few Norse rune stones which have been found in Greenland.[188]

In other words, when someone does something, there is evidence of it. For every action there is a reaction! This is why the case is very different for the historical veracity of the Bible.

Since there is so much archaeological evidence of biblical ancient Greece, biblical ancient Jerusalem, and Ancient Near East (ANE) in general, from ancient ruins the whole way down to ancient coins and pottery, it is easy to not only believe the events in history that took place, but one can take a leap back in time and understand certain things with precision when literally visiting these sites for himself. Not so with Mormon history. Since there is no credible or realistic archaeological evidence of Mormon history, it is not only impossible to verify that the events written in the *Book of Mormon* took place, but is also hard to put any type of credit into the *Book of Mormon* because of this fact. The same logic can be used for the History in the Bible. Because we "see" the history that took place, the Bible has strong argumentation from archaeological validity to say the least.

---

[188]The Department of Anthropology Smithsonian Institution. *Inquiry concerning the Smithsonian Institution's alleged use of the Book of Mormon as a scientific guide.* (National Museum of Natural History Smithsonian Institution., 1996). https://www.mrm.org/smithsonian

Ancient Artifacts

Let's dive right in to discuss and analyze some of the archaeological evidence discovered in modern times that date back to the first few centuries AD. We begin with an ancient inscription, which is the Dedication Inscription of Pontius Pilate. Pontius Pilate was the person that ultimately had Jesus crucified. Pontius Pilate was the procurator of Judea.[189]

In John chapter eighteen, starting at verse twenty-eight, after the Jews captured Jesus and put him before Pilate to be judged, Pontius Pilate came out to them and asked what charges they were bringing against this man.[190] The Jews told him that if he were not a criminal, they would not have brought Jesus to him, implying that Pilate should just trust their judgment. Since the Jews at that time had no right to execute Jesus, it seems they thought that it was something that must be laid in the hands of Pontius Pilate. After Jesus and Pontius Pilate had a discussion on Jesus' identity,[191] Pilate eventually had Jesus brutally flogged and finally crucified on a cross.[192]

Now that we have a good idea of who Pontius Pilate is, historically speaking, let's look at the Pontius Pilate Inscription, which is direct evidence of Pilate's existence.

> During the excavation of the Roman Theater at Caesarea, a stone was found in the landing of a flight of steps. It bears the inscription "To the people of Caesarea Tiberium Pontius Pilate Prefect of Judea." Another line seems to indicate the word meaning "dedication." It is

---

[189]Flavius Josephus and William Whiston, *The Works of Josephus: Complete and Unabridged* (Peabody: Hendrickson, 1996, c1987), Ant 18.55.

[190]See Jn. 18:29.

[191]See Jn. 18:33–38.

[192]See Jn. 19:16–27

likely that the stone was originally placed on an outside wall to commemorate the theater's construction.[193]

So, there is a considerable amount of literary evidence from the book of John and from the writings of Josephus that we have seen, but there are also several other writings not mentioned here that contain information about Pontius Pilate.[194]

There has been "no physical evidence [of the existence of Pontius Pilate] until 1961, when archaeologists discovered the inscription [of Pilate] on a stone [described above which] dated to the period from AD 26 to 37."[195] With this in mind, one can see that there is enough evidence, both in literary sources and through this inscription, to believe that Pontius Pilate was a real person at the time of Christ. "The inscription further substantiates the existence and position of this Roman who played a pivotal, though unfortunate, role in the plan of God for the Messiah Jesus."[196]

Next, we turn to an ancient mosaic. Mosaics are a form of art, which consist of taking small fragments of stone or other materials and placing them against a wall, floor, or other flat, hard surface which are cemented into place to create a picture of things, places, words, designs or people, etc. The *Megiddo Mosaic Inscription* is of superior significance for a couple of reasons, but we should first understand what the inscription describes.

The massive mosaic describes a table offered to Christ by a female worshipper named "Akeptous." The ornate Greek inscription refers

---

[193]Ralph Muncaster, *Can Archaeology Prove the New Testament?* (Eugene: Harvest House Publishers, 2000) 36.

[194]See also Tertullian, Eusebius, Philo, Tacitus, and Agapius of Hierapolis (Joseph Holden and Norman Geisler, *The Popular Handbook of Archaeology* (Eugene: Harvest House Publishers, 2013), 345; not to mention the other three gospels found in the New Testament.

[195]Joseph Holden and Norman Geisler, *The Popular Handbook of Archaeology* (Eugene: Harvest House Publishers, 2013) 347.

[196]Ibid. 348.

"to the God Jesus Christ" and that the table was offered to Jesus "as a memorial." The phrase "God Jesus Christ" has been over-lined for emphasis.[197]

The location of this mosaic offers the notion that Christianity has spread locally, as well as that it was accepted by people who have heard the message of Christ, early on; in fact, in the third century AD. Now, another notable thing about this description is the fact that it shows that people worshiped Jesus as God. In other words, they affirmed his deity.[198] The reason this is significant is because the Bible speaks openly and boldly of Jesus' deity, with the understanding that he is God and should be worshiped.[199] The fact that this mosaic exists and was local to the events of Christ as well as the time that it happened, points to the fact that the true message of the gospel was not dissolved or distorted because people genuinely believed their eye-witness ancestors. In any event, worshipers of Jesus seek to bring him glory in modern times as well as ancient times, which is why we find artifacts as such.

Next, we can discuss an ancient graffiti. It is common throughout history for people to vandalize buildings. A person can travel to Italy today, visit the famous Roman Colosseum and see the type of vandalism that appeared in that period. Most of the graffiti was carved onto the side of a wall depicting anything from fighting gladiators to caricatures to words of protest, etc. In one instance in Rome, "A caricature scratched on the wall of the Palatine palace in Rome, and dating back to the third century, represents a human figure with an ass's head, hanging upon a cross, while a man stands before it in the attitude of worship. Under the effigy is this ill-spelled inscription: 'Alexamenos adores his God.'"[200]

---

[197]Ibid. 308.

[198]Ibid.

[199]See Mt. 2:2; 14:33; 28:9; Jn. 1:1; 1:14; 9:38; 10:30; 20:28; Col. 1:16; 2:9; Heb. 1:1–8; et al.

[200]Augustus Hopkins Strong, *Systematic Theology* (Bellingham, Wa.: Logos Research Systems, Inc., 2004). 314.

This graffiti is known as the *Alexamenos Graffito*, which is significant not only because it is the oldest known representation of the crucifix, "which was a mock-picture from the hand of a heathen— an excellent illustration of the word of Paul that the preaching of Christ crucified is foolishness to the Greeks,"[201] but it is also significant because it shows that the crucifixion was really used since the actual crucifixion must come before the graffiti itself. In other words, this type of poking fun would not be anything unless there was some truth to it. "It can scarcely be doubted that we have here a contemporary caricature, executed by one of the Praetorian Guard, ridiculing the faith of a Christian."[202]

So, it is quite significant to the argument for the cross because it was performed by one who was clearly not a Christian. "We know that in the second century, the Christians were charged with the worship of an ass, and that at that time there were already Christians in the imperial palace."[203] It appears that there must have been some type of cultural behavior that made fun of Christians because it was also understood to have been a type of persecution that the Jews endured as well.[204]

So, then, the *Alexamenos Graffito* "supports the gospel statements describing the crucifixion as the manner by which Christ died, a method of capital punishment that has previously been disputed."[205] In any event, the people, things, and events surrounding the life of Jesus are clearly real, so what reason is there to doubt the rest of it? Let us continue, however, our journey through the world of the first few centuries in Christian history before we get to that.

---

[201]Philip Schaff and David Schley Schaff, *History of the Christian Church* (Oak Harbor, WA: Logos Research Systems, Inc., 1997).

[202]M.G. Easton, *Easton's Bible Dictionary* (Oak Harbor, WA: Logos Research Systems, Inc., 1996, c1897).

[203]Philip Schaff and David Schley Schaff, *History of the Christian Church* (Oak Harbor, WA: Logos Research Systems, Inc., 1997).

[204]Ibid.

[205]Joseph Holden and Norman Geisler, *The Popular Handbook of Archaeology*, 309.

The final archaeological discovery that we will discuss is an ossuary. An ossuary is basically the ancient equivalent to our modern-day casket, but only held the bones of the deceased and not the entire body. Ossuaries were hewn from stone, and sometimes had very ornate designs on them depending on whose bones were actually in the box. They were normally very small because they would only contain bones, not intact skeletons, and for obvious reasons, such as they were easy to store and easy to move.

There have been several ossuaries found from the ancient times, and there are definitely a few that stand out from among the rest. Here, we discuss the *James Ossuary*, which is supposedly the bone box of James, who was the brother of Jesus. The significance of this ossuary is almost obvious: that, for one, we have a testimony of Jesus' family, and second, that the time Jesus existed is in line with historical documents and other evidence.[206]

So, now that we understand the value of the bone box, that James was the brother of Jesus according to the Bible as well as according to Flavius Josephus,[207] we can move on to the issue of whether or not the ancient relic is fraudulent or not.

It is believed by some that the bone box's inscription, which attests to *James, the son of Joseph, the brother of Jesus*, that it is a modern forgery as alluded to above. An argument against the authenticity of the James Ossuary is that "Though the bone box itself and the first half of the inscription are not contested, arguments that the second half of the inscription ("brother of Jesus") was recently engraved (as a forgery) and was not completed by the same hand have been posited due to the absence of natural occurring patina."[208] The argument could be defeated, one would think, "If the same consistency of the patina

---

[206]Joseph Holden and Norman Geisler, *The Popular Handbook of Archaeology,* 309.

[207]See Gal. 1:9, et al.; Flavius Josephus and William Whiston, *The Works of Josephus: Complete and Unabridged* (Peabody: Hendrickson, 1996, c1987), Antiquities 20.200.

[208]Joseph Holden and Norman Geisler, *The Popular Handbook of Archaeology,* 312.

is equally distributed on the ossuary and found within the engraved grooves."[209]

The Geological Survey of Israel certified that the patina that was found in the engravings of the ossuary was the same as the patina found on the side of the ossuary.[210] So, what this means is that the patina, which was developed through great lengths of time, is not only on the places surrounding the inscription, but the same patina is also in the inscription. It was also believed, as mentioned above, that the second half of the inscription was later added, but both inscriptions were examined, and both were found to have had the same consistent patina. Thanks to modern technology, we can conclude that the ossuary is authentic.

Another important thing to note is that neither the buyer nor seller realized the value of what was being bought and sold.[211] The seller sold it for a few hundred dollars, which is the ordinary price for something like that.[212] On top of that, the owner of the James Ossuary "did not regard it as important enough to have it on display with other major items in his collection."[213] With these in mind, it is beyond reasonable doubt that the James Ossuary is absolutely authentic.

Because the James Ossuary has fell under so much scrutiny (in courtrooms, under microscopes, and through the bifocals of several paleographers), it can be considered the most authenticated artifact in history.[214] In other words, the fact that someone accused the ossuary to be a forgery made it even more under a microscope, so to speak, than it would have been if it were instantly accepted as authentic.

---

[209]Ibid.

[210]Hershel Shanks and Ben Witherington III, *The Brother of Jesus: The dramatic story & meaning of the first archaeological link to Jesus & His family* (New York: HarperCollins Publishers, 2003) 48.

[211]Ibid. 49.

[212]Ibid.

[213]Ibid.

[214]Joseph Holden and Norman Geisler, *The Popular Handbook of Archaeology*, 315.

Archaeology does not offer anything like these things discussed above for the *Book of Mormon*. The problem is that though the *Book of Mormon* mentions cities, steel tools, weapons, and great wars being fought, there has not been a shred of archaeological evidence discovered. One would think that there would be swords, shields, javelins, and coins found, among others, but there has not been a single thing ever located. Which, this seems to throw very large red flags concerning not only the historicity of the book, but also the veracity of Mormonism all together.

What does this say about the credibility of the *Doctrine and Covenants*, where the doctrine of exaltation is found? Some might try to argue that this question is committing the *genetic fallacy* but remember that these claims are all coming from the same person, which question one's character and motivation. T. Edward Damer suggests in his book, *Attacking Faulty Reasoning*:

A premise should be acceptable to a mature, rational person if it expresses any of the following:

1. A claim that is well established and generally undisputed by the community of competent inquirers.
2. A claim that is confirmed by one's personal observation or by an uncontroverted testimony of another competent observer.
3. A claim that is adequately defended in the context of the argument.
4. An uncontroverted claim by a relevant authority.
5. The conclusion of another good argument.
6. A relatively minor claim that seems to be a reasonable assumption in the context of the argument.[215]

---

[215]T. Edward Damer, *Attacking Faulty Reasoning: A practical guide to fallacy-free arguments 7th edition* (Boston: Wadsworth, 2013), 36.

Regarding specifically the doctrine of exaltation (found in the *Doctrine and Covenants* et al.) in light of these guidelines for acceptance, it could easily be argued that it fails all of these. The implicit claim of the Law of the gods is highly disputed as we have seen with the testimonies from the Nauvoo Expositor. It is unconfirmed and controverted. It is not adequately defended, and the authority of Joseph Smith is highly questionable, as we saw in chapter three It is not the conclusion of another good argument, and it is not a minor claim that seems to be a reasonable assumption in context. Damer continues, "Eyewitness reports, however, are notoriously problematic. Experience tells us that there is good reason to be skeptical about many of them."[216] Damer here is referring to a single eyewitness report, much like that of Joseph Smith. He goes on to mention that multiple eyewitnesses will give wildly different reports of the same event but should be accepted if they do not contradict one another.[217] We have therefore, logically, theologically, philosophically, and archaeologically speaking, good reason to question such claims of Joseph Smith.

Summary

Archaeology has something objective to say, which is that nothing lines up with the claims of the *Book of Mormon*, but on the other hand, things do line up with what one finds in the Bible. All this to show that the *Book of Mormon* is not credible. And, since it is not credible, then why would anyone consider the *Doctrine and Covenants*, where the doctrine of exaltation is found, to be credible since it was written by the same author. This all may rightly place a heavy anxiety on the one who believes that the Law of the gods corresponds to reality.

---

[216]Ibid.

[217]Ibid. See also 1 Cor. 15:3–8.

Chapter Six:

A Biblical and Logical Defense of Christianity Against Mormonism

"Heaven and earth shall pass away, but my words shall not pass away." ~ Matthew 24:35

THERE IS A reason the Bible is the world's number one best seller, and it is not only because it is the only source of where one finds real hope, but also because the truth it contains about reality is not only attractive but also tested as we have seen in several examples in the previous chapter. Unlike the teachings of the gods of ancient Rome, Greece, Mormons, and the Vikings, the Bible stands firm through the tests of time, unlike other sacred texts because it teaches the truth about Jesus, life, God, the afterlife, sin, and ultimate reality.

The Bible, this paper *library* (collection of books) that is "sharper than any two-edged sword,"[1] will lay open all that rests on the butcher's table for the butcher to see the contents of what is inside. Namely, "piercing even to the dividing asunder of soul and spirit, and of the joints and marrow, and is a discerner of the thoughts and intents of the heart."[218] With its many pages, the Bible itself reveals to a person what he or she is made of; it brings the message of hope to the hopeless through Jesus; it is a mirror for those who want to see what they look

---

[218]Heb. 4:13.

like in the eyes of his or her Creator; and it stands true among all other sacred texts and interpretations.

Mormonism attacks these ideas using the phrase, *restored gospel*, which essentially claims to be the catapult for the existence of Mormonism:

> God's reestablishment of the truths and ordinances of His gospel among men on earth. *The gospel of Jesus Christ was lost from the earth through the apostasy that took place following the earthly ministry of Christ's Apostles. That apostasy made necessary the Restoration of the gospel.* Through visions, the ministering of angels, and revelations to men on the earth, *God restored the gospel.* The Restoration started with the Prophet Joseph Smith (JS—H 1; D&C 128:20–21) and has continued to the present through the work of the Lord's living prophets.[219]

There is no *restored gospel* because the true Church never died. Jesus said that "Heaven and earth shall pass away, but my words shall not pass away,"[220] which is the exact opposite of what Mormonism teaches here. The only way they could be logically consistent and get away with saying this is by saying that what the Bible records Jesus saying in the above verse is corrupted. But also, the following biblical passage must be corrupted as well, in order for the *restored gospel* to be true:

---

[219]The Church of Jesus Christ of the Latter-day Saints. *Guide to the Scriptures.* (Utah: The Church of Jesus Christ of the Latter-day Saints. Intellectual Reserve, Incorporated. 2013); emphasis added. https://www.churchofjesuschrist.org/study/scriptures/gs/introduction?lang=eng.

[220]Mt. 24:35.

He saith unto them, "But whom say ye that I am?" And Simon Peter answered and said, "Thou art the Christ, the Son of the living God." And Jesus answered and said unto him, "Blessed art thou, Simon Barjona: for flesh and blood hath not revealed it unto thee, but my Father which is in heaven. And I say also unto thee, That thou art Peter, and upon this rock I will build my church; and the gates of hell shall not prevail against it. And I will give unto thee the keys of the kingdom of heaven: and whatsoever thou shalt bind on earth shall be bound in heaven: and whatsoever thou shalt loose on earth shall be loosed in heaven."[221]

So, Jesus says that on this rock-solid statement made by Peter, that His Church will be built on the *Son of the living God*, and because of such, *the gates of hell will not prevail against His Church*. So, the ultimate question is, why did Mormonism even ever need to happen in the first place if it is built around the idea that the gospel needed to be restored?[222] It was never lost; it was never corrupted, and it was never absent or on sabbatical. The problem is that Mormons could not possibly point to a place in history where the true Church started to become corrupt, let alone the Bible. All this to show that there are several issues with the idea that the Bible, which accurately describes God, has been corrupted.

Earlier, I made the claim that the Bible is true. The reason the Bible is true is because Jesus is God and the Bible is the Word of God, and He says that it is true.[223] We can read about his miracles and know that he is God. He created sight in a man born blind, just like God created

---

[221]Mt. 16:15–19.

[222]Also, why even call the Bible one of the four sacred texts of Mormonism if it is so "corrupted"?

[223]See Jn. 17:17.

the heavens and the earth.[224] He fed the four thousand and then the five thousand, creating food for people out of nowhere, like God did for the Israelites while wandering in the desert.[225] These are just a few examples of several, but the idea is that we can know that they are true because of the testimony of Jesus' disciples and the witness of the Holy Spirit. So, if Jesus is God (which he is), and God's Word cannot be corrupted (which it cannot be), and Jesus explains that his Church will never take a sabbatical or apostatize (which it does not), then it is safe to assume that what Jesus says about his Church is true.

The Bible has not been changed through time as one can clearly understand from an analysis of the extant manuscripts that are available in museums across the world and in digital photographs on internet archives and libraries.[226] Mormons have neither been able to prove that the Bible has been corrupted nor show which parts have been corrupted. There is a reason for this. There are over twenty-five thousand, hand-written manuscripts of the New Testament from the old world, with almost six thousand of that number being in the original autographical language of *Koine* Greek.[227] With this high number of manuscripts, they can be hypothetically (and literally) placed side by side in order to be examined. When side by side, every word can be compared to one another from manuscript to manuscript. There are slight differences in the manuscripts that are from the old world, but none of these *variants*

---

[224]See Gen. 1 and Jn. 9.

[225]See Mk. 8, Jn. 6, and Ex. 16.

[226]For instance, see *The Center for the study of New Testament Manuscripts* (CSNTM). https://www.csntm.org/.

[227]Norman Geisler and Joseph M. Holden. *The Popular Handbook of Archaeology and the Bible* (Eugene: Harvest House Publishers, 2013), 122; Craig Blomberg. *The Historical Reliability of the New Testament* (Nashville: B&H Academic, 2016), 613.

(slight differences), make a difference in any of the doctrinal material that is in the New Testament.[228]

The New Testament, then, as much as it has been copied, has proof that it has not changed (contrary to the claims of Mormonism) because we can see these documents laid out before us through the span of time, so to speak, and analyze the manuscripts from the second century forward, and because of such, we can know that it has not been changed since the original autographs with up to "99.9 percent accuracy on anything of real concern."[229] We can see from beginning to end, in a sense, these manuscripts which span time and see that the New Testament itself does not change. This is significant because we have a solid foundation to work from in translating the original language into our own modern language, namely, English, as well as that there are no doctrines in Christianity that have been altered since the beginning of Christianity. There is no need and no possibility for a "restored gospel."

In order for Jesus to be the same yesterday, today, and forever, it would also mean that his Word would have to be the same, yesterday, today and forever.[230] Therefore the Christian scriptural foundation, the Word of God, is so powerful and influential because it simply does not change. It is noteworthy at this moment to again point out that Jesus says, "Heaven and earth shall pass away, but my words shall not pass away."[231] Not only is this *not* the case for Mormon scripture (their words do pass away, e. g., blacks entering into the priesthood and the issue of polygamy), but it *is* the case for the Bible, which ultimately means that there is no need for scripture beyond the Bible (which is

---

[228]Norman Geisler and William L. Nix. *From God to us: How we got our Bible* (Chicago: Moody Publishers, 2012), 243.

[229]Geisler and Holden, 127.

[230]See Heb. 13:8.

[231]Mt. 24:35; Interestingly, this verse alone disproves Mormonism from a biblical Christian perspective, since because Jesus said this, there is no need for a "restored gospel," which is the whole motivation for the invention of Mormonism; see also Mt. 16:17–18.

what Mormon scripture and sources are) because Jesus' words will not pass away. Jesus is the ultimate authority of canonicity. The Bible is true because he is the truth.[232]

Something else to consider is that there is even a translation of the Bible written from the Mormon perspective. We will look at a comparison of John chapter one, verse one, in the Koine Greek translation of the New Testament and the *King James Version*, which is the standard biblical text for Mormons in order to compare with the Joseph Smith Translation. In the Greek New Testament, we read: Ἐν ἀρχῇ ἦν ὁ λόγος, καὶ ὁ λόγος ἦν πρὸς τὸν θεόν, καὶ θεὸς ἦν ὁ λόγος.[233]

The *King James Version* translates this same verse as "In the beginning was the Word, and the Word was with God, and the Word was God."[234] Even a verbatim translation (which one should probably never do, but I digress) of the Koine Greek of the same verse would not read very differently than what the *King James Version* reads: "In beginning was the Word, and the Word was with God, and God was the Word."[235] Both a verbatim translation and the *King James Version* of John chapter one, verse one, contain the same *idea* in them. Primarily, for our purposes, that the *Logos* (*the Word*, i.e., *Jesus*) *is God*. This verse both directly *and* indirectly claims that the Word (*Logos*) is God. We have already seen how this verse directly states that the Word (*Logos*) is God, and indirectly, through the beginning clause of the verse makes the claim that the Word (*Logos*) existed before the beginning. In other words, this verse says that the Word (*Logos*) already existed before time began.

Now that we have this information established, we can look at the *Joseph Smith Translation*, named for the founder of the Latter-day Saint Movement (which began in the nineteenth century). It reads in

---

[232]See Jn. 14:6.

[233]Kurt Aland et al., *The Greek New Testament, Fourth Revised Edition (with Morphology)* (Deutsche Bibelgesellschaft, 1993; 2006), Jn. 1:1.

[234]Jn. 1:1.

[235]Author's verbatim translation.

John chapter one, verse one: "In the beginning was the gospel preached through the Son. And the gospel was the word and the word was with the Son, and the Son was with God, and the Son was of God."[236] As the reader can clearly see, there is a great deal of difference between this and the same verse in the *King James Version* of the Bible. What is interesting is that the Mormon church claims that "The JST to some extent assists in restoring the plain and precious things that have been lost from the Bible."[237] So, the claim is that the *King James Version* has been corrupted, and the *Joseph Smith Translation* is an attempt to restore those things that were lost.

Not only are the words in this example drastically changed, but also the idea is very different as well as confusing: "In the beginning was the gospel preached through the Son." To whom was the gospel preached? To God? What exactly is the word, *word,* referring to, that is mentioned in the Joseph Smith translation of this verse? It is clear what it refers to in the Greek and the *King James Version*, but not in the *Joseph Smith Translation*. On top of this, the *Joseph Smith Translation* says that the Son was *of* God. It seems safe to assume that Joseph Smith had *another Jesus* in his mind when he refers to the "Son." But the problem is, the earliest manuscripts (and manuscripts in the centuries following) do not teach that the Word (λόγος) was *of* God but that the Word *was* God. Being *of God* opens a whole other world of definition to what that can mean exactly. This seems to be a pragmatic translation for Joseph Smith. It *works* for him to be able to not only change meaning of the true text, but also to manipulate his future followers. The text continues in verse four and clarifies some things about the first verse in the *Joseph Smith Translation*: "In Him was the gospel and the

[236]Joseph Smith, *Joseph Smith Translation of the Bible* (Published by the Church of Jesus Christ of Latter-day Saints. Joseph Smith, I.L. Rogers, E. Robinson, publishing committee). 1867. John 1:1.

[237]Joseph Smith, *Joseph Smith Translation of the Bible* (Published by the Church of Jesus Christ of Latter-day Saints. Joseph Smith, I.L. Rogers, E. Robinson, publishing committee). 1867. https://www.churchofjesuschrist.org/study/scriptures/bd/joseph-smith-translation?lang=eng.

gospel was the life, and the life was the light of men."[238] So now we know better about what the "gospel" is, which is different than the Son, but not from the *word*. Then the *Son* and the *word* are two different things, but not necessarily the *word* and the *gospel*. This gives Joseph Smith more room to confuse his readers. It makes his use of the word, *Jesus*, a manipulation.

For instance, if Jesus, *the Son*, is not the ultimate authority, which is what his translation teaches, then Jesus is of less authority and power than the Father, ultimately making the Mormon Jesus not the Supreme Being. There are several issues with Jesus not being God. Number one, the *King James Version* of the Bible (one of their claimed holy scriptures) teaches that Jesus is God.[239] Second, theology and logic teach that if Jesus was not God, then he would not be sinless, and therefore, would not be a sufficient sacrifice for human sin. Third, if Jesus was not God, he could not forgive sins. Fourth, if Jesus is not Deity, then why does the book of Hebrews teach that he is above angels and Moses, and if he is neither an angel nor Moses, then who is he? These issues among others show that the Mormon Jesus is insufficient for salvation. Paul teaches us that there is no other gospel, but only one.[240]

John chapter one, verses one through three in the *King James Version* creates a huge problem for Mormon beliefs, which is why Joseph Smith likely made his own translation so dizzying. The stance that the Latter-day Saint church now takes is that "while some believe the three members of the Trinity are of one substance, Latter-day Saints believe they are three physically separate beings, but fully one in love, purpose and will."[241] Notice what is said here: *Three physically sepa-*

---

[238] *Joseph Smith Translation.* John 1:4.

[239] See Jn. 8:58; 10:30; 20:28; Mk. 10:18; Col. 1:19; 2:9; Heb. 1:8; Rev. 1:8, 17–18; et al.

[240] See Gal. 1:6–9.

[241] The Church of Jesus Christ of the Latter-day Saints. *Godhead.* (The Church of Jesus Christ of the Latter-day Saints: Newsroom) https://newsroom.churchofjesuschrist.org/article/godhead.

rate beings.... One of the main issues here is that Mormons claim that the *King James Version* of the Bible is one of their sacred sources. It seems likely at this point that the only reason Joseph Smith made the *King James Version* of the Bible one of the Mormon sacred texts was to make Mormonism more palatable to non-Mormons.

So, the Bible remains true, even though there are several issues of corruption in translation coming from Mormonism, which tries to change the position of Jesus deity and accuse biblical Christians of changing it originally. We can therefore see the unchanging nature of the Bible.

Of these two English translations of John, chapter one (the *King James Version*, and the *Joseph Smith Translation*), one of them claims that Jesus is God, and one claims that he is not God. As we will discover in the next few pages, both of these claims cannot be true: Either Jesus is God, or he is not God.

If Christianity Is True, Then Mormonism Is False

The Bible is exclusive in what it teaches. This means that there are no other options. Jesus says, "I am the way, the truth, and the life; no one comes to the Father but through me."[242] Christianity is exclusive soteriologically speaking. This mean that Christianity claims to be the only correct religion. The issue is that all other religions also teach exclusive soteriology. They all claim to be the one correct path to salvation.

Concerning the *Book of Mormon*, again for instance, Joseph Smith teaches that "I told the brethren that the *Book of Mormon* was the most correct of any book on earth, and the keystone of our religion, and a man would get nearer to God by abiding by its precepts, than by any

---

[242]See Jn. 14:6.

other book."[243] Yet, the *Book of Mormon* teaches that a person is saved by works and not by faith: "For we know that it is by grace that we are saved, after all we can do."[244] The irony about this is that it is an act of plagiarism yet disagrees with what is plagiarized. Remember, the *King James Version* of the Bible says in Ephesians chapter two, verses eight and nine, "For by grace are ye saved through faith; and that not of yourselves: it is the gift of God: Not of works, lest any man should boast."[245] Therefore, ironically, Mormonism teaches that it is an exclusive religion as well; that Mormonism alone ("the restored gospel") has the answers to the questions of life. But if the *Book of Mormon* is the most correct book of any on earth, then why are there so many important unanswered questions such as, why does it so awkwardly claim that after a man who had his head cut off, tried to take a breath, even after doing a push-up (also while headless)?[246] Why was the Book of Mormon written in an expired language style? As far as archeology is concerned, why also does the *Book of Mormon* mention wars with millions of people and nothing evidential has ever been found to verify its claims? The reason is because the *Book of Mormon* is a false writing. If it were true, there would be archaeological evidence in the State of New York, where a majority of the events within the *Book of Mormon* take place.

In any event, the nature of the sheer existence of all religions implies that they are exclusive. Exclusivity does not need to be spelled out for all religions because all religions are essentially making the claim that they have the answer to the problems and questions of life, therefore all are exclusive, even Hinduism, which is polytheistic and postmodern to an extreme.

---

[243]Joseph Smith, *History of the Church of Jesus Christ of the Latter-day Saints*. (Brigham Young University Studies, Deseret Book Company, 1948) Volume 4, chapter 27. https://byustudies.byu.edu/content/volume-4-chapter-27.

[244]Joseph Smith, *Book of Mormon*. 2 Nephi 25:23.

[245]Eph. 2:8–9.

[246]Joseph Smith, *Book of Mormon*, Ether 15:31.

The idea is that not all religions can be true, but there can only be one that is true, if even any at all. The law of non-contradiction teaches that A cannot be −A. In other words, contradictory statements cannot both be true in the same sense at the same time. For instance, the claim that Jesus is God cannot be equal to the claim that Jesus is not God (A ≠ −A). Likewise, because all religions claim to be exclusive by their very nature (by their sheer existence), they cannot all be correct. We examine the claims of each and rule out the ones that are wrong, absurd, or simply lies, and we hold fast to that which is true.[247]

All religions can logically be false, but not all of them can logically be true. One religion can logically be true, which is what I argue for Christianity, but not all of them can be true because they all oppose one another. Not even two of them can be true, because by their existence, they fundamentally oppose one another. Would a religion need to exist if it thought another religion were the truth? Consider what is likely the most extreme example: Hinduism teaches that "there are almost no restrictions on personal beliefs, but in order to qualify as a Hindu, a religion has to (1) regard the *Vedas* as divinely inspired and authoritative, (2) accept the caste system, and (3) respect the veneration of the various levels of deities and spirits, including the protection of cows."[248] Notice the wording in this citation: not that a *person* must do these things to qualify, but a *religion* must do these three things to qualify as Hinduism. The reason Hinduism is such an extreme example is because it is a polytheistic religion, having up to three hundred and thirty million gods (to help wrap your mind around this, there are approximately 330,150,668 people in the United States), and also because Hinduism teaches that just about all religions are *true*.

When I traveled to India recently, there were literally cows walking down the street like they owned the place. People walked past them as if they were walking past a human being. Why such strange behavior?

---

[247]See 1 Thess. 5:21.

[248]Winfried Corduan, *Neighboring Faiths: A Christian Introduction to World Religions* (Downers Grove: InterVarsity Press, 2012), 267.

Because many Hindus believe that their grandmother's spirit could be in the cow. What gave them such an idea is a longer story for which we do not have time for here, but it is clear that when one visits India, Hinduism is alive and well, even in regard to the caste system, no matter what one is told about it in mainstream media. The point here is that this behavior and belief is very different from other religions, such as those which condone the consumption of beef. It is either wrong to consume beef or it is not wrong.

But since Hinduism teaches that all or most religions are potentially true, it seems that this is the most extreme example to show that all religions by their own existence claim exclusivity. If all religions are true, then why does Hinduism exist? What is the point of it? It seems that in this case, Hinduism just adds to the plethora of confusion in religion and should rightly be dismissed as not only false, but also counterproductive. The point is Hinduism claims exclusivity *because* it exists. It says that Hinduism is *the way*,[249] which ultimately is every way and any way.

Since all religions by their sheer existence imply that they are the *correct way* (which is the case, even in our extreme example of Hinduism), then they cannot all be true. The reason they cannot all be true is because they all go in different directions. If one wanted to travel across the United States, would he use just any map—perhaps the map of the Pittsburgh Zoo, for instance? Or would he use a map specifically for the United States? Hopefully, the latter. If one wanted to travel from Philadelphia to San Francisco, a map detailing the route from Athens, Greece to Madrid, Spain would not get him there. Similarly, just because there are a bunch of religions that claim to know and show the truth about reality does not mean that any of them are absolutely true.

So, *by their existence*, every religion disagrees with the other religions that are not themselves. This is simply considering the

---

[249]Here, we could also have a lengthy discussion on *Daoism* as well.

fundamental Law of Identity. For instance, if Mormonism agreed with Christianity on all parts, then how would one be able to tell them apart?[250] What would be the difference if there were no differences? The fact is that these religions do disagree with one another, which is why we know them separately as Mormonism and Christianity, and not simply one or the other. The reason we can tell Mormonism apart from Christianity is *because* of their differences.

Take the example of Jesus, for instance. Some religions say that Jesus never existed; some religions say that he never died (which assumes his existence); some religions maintain that when Jesus died, his body disappeared in a cloud of gasses, into thin air; some teach that he was just a good man and nothing more; some hold that he did not do miracles; some teach he did do miracles; some teach that he died and rose again; others teach that his body was stolen or hidden; some teach that he is the Son of God; some that he is not the Son of God. Christianity teaches that Jesus is God in the flesh, but many religions do not, and the list goes on. In view of the law of non-contradiction,[251] we can know that each one of these claims cannot be both true and false at the same time and in the same sense. The claim that "*Jesus did miracles*," cannot be both true *and* false. But it is either true *or* false. We can know that this claim is true *beyond reasonable doubt* by reading the Bible and examining the evidence therein. We can likewise know that the claim that "Jesus did not do miracles" is false, based on the evidence contrary to the claim.

This is ultimately how one can discover whether or not a specific religion is true beyond a reasonable doubt. If one examines the different religions and find false claims, especially in regarding the central objects of such a religion as well as claims regarding the beginnings of such a religion, then he can assume that such a religion is false. If one examines Christianity, for instance, and finds that the claims made

---

[250]Similarly, God cannot create another God equal to Himself. If He did, then how could one tell them apart? This is again, a simple violation of the law of identity.

[251]This fundamental law of logic which cannot be discussed enough.

are based on historical events, then from this he can know that it is true beyond a reasonable doubt. Unfortunately for Mormonism, this is not the case.

Since I have demonstrated that there cannot be more than one *ultimately true religion*, we can know that the Bible is true through an examination of the scriptures. The reason we discuss this here is because again it is considered by Mormons to be one of their sacred documents. In any event, we look at the contents of it historically, archaeologically, and logically, for a few reasons. Logically, we can examine the scriptures and see that the stories in the Bible do not appear to be embellished: there are no talking crosses and heads that reach up to heaven.[252] The stories of the Bible play out naturally, and where the miracles are communicated in the Bible, we do not find them to be illogical or absurd, such as trying to breathe without a head as found in the *Book of Mormon*. For instance, in comparison to Matthew chapter fourteen, where Jesus walked on the water, we do not find elsewhere in the Bible that Jesus made square circles or that he explained the smell of the color of red. The things mentioned in the Bible are not logically impossible but are as if someone witnessed these things and recorded them naturally.

Historically and archaeologically speaking, among other things, one can read the Bible and know that it is true because many of the names of the cities in the Bible still exist today, and he can even go and visit them. The Bible records the accounts often in such detail that it would not make sense to record them in such detail unless these things were actually part of the experiences of the biblical writers. The authors of, "*I Don't Have Enough Faith to Be an Atheist*" make a lot of sense: "Now, why would Luke be so accurate with trivial details like wind direction, water depths, and peculiar town names, but not

---

[252]William Hone, *The Lost Books of the Bible: The Gospel According to Peter* (New York: Gramercy Books, 1979), 285.

be accurate when it comes to important events like miracles?"[253] The point here is that if all of the city names are found to be correct and details surrounding these things, why would we not assume that the author is telling the truth on the other more remarkable details of what he has written.

Archaeologically speaking, unlike the claims of the *Book of Mormon* as mentioned above, there are archaeological artifacts found in museums literally all over the world excavated from biblically described times and places. There are artifacts and evidence ranging from tombs to inscriptions,[254] to weapons, to boats, to clothing, to tools, to coins, and pottery (let alone twenty-five thousand manuscripts), to name a very small number of things. One can see these things at a museum, often in his own city. A person can even visit ancient cities that are mentioned in the Bible and see some of these things from the time of Jesus and see that they corroborate with the claims in the Bible, which gives strong support for the veracity of the Bible.

We should also consider the veracity of the Bible through a spiritual lens. In John chapter sixteen, Jesus tells us that the Holy Spirit will convict the world in regard to sin and righteousness and judgment.[255] This means that the Holy Spirit, the one Jesus calls the "Spirit of Truth" a few verses later,[256] has access to the inner being of a person and therefore can reveal the truth about Jesus and the words of the Bible to a person. It is not only this inner moving of the Holy Spirit which increases one's Christian faith, however, but it is all of these things together that equates to the sum of *evidence-based faith*, as opposed to *blind faith*. The Bible is ultimately one place where Mormons and

---

[253]Norman Geisler and Frank Turek, *I Don't Have Enough Faith to Be an Atheist* (Wheaton: Crossway, 2004), 260.

[254]See Nace Howell, *The Erastus Inscription: What does it mean?* Apologetics and Evidence: January, 2015. https://apologeticsandevidence.blogspot.com/2015/01/the-erastus-inscription-what-does-it.html.

[255]See Jn. 16:8.

[256]See Jn. 16:13.

Christians have some common ground. As a primary and sacred source for Mormons, the Bible is simply more than the credit they ascribe it.

A True Faith from a True Text

One is a Christian because Christianity is *true*. Not because his parents were Christians or because he was born in the United States of America or because it is true for him, but because he knows that there is something rather than nothing, that God exists. A One is a Christian because he knows that there is sin in his life, and because he can know that the greatest miracle (creation) provides the possibility of all other miracles, many of which are recorded in the Bible.[257] Therefore, both Mormons and Christians (and everyone else) can read what the Bible says and know that the human authors who wrote such things down were not out of their minds but actually were eyewitnesses to the events. We discover many truths about reality through the text.

Even more, it seems that if any person saw what the biblical human authors witnessed, he or she would end up in the same boat, so to speak. What is meant by this is that there was an element of trauma that must have been experienced by the disciples. It is common knowledge that many, if not most, of the Apostles of Christ were martyred. Now the question is, "Why were they martyred?" It seems that the cause boils down to the things that they witnessed and experienced. They saw things like people being healed from blindness from birth, a man turned water turn into wine, and he walked on the water as mentioned above. People saw this same man raise people from the dead. What is more, they saw him die and rise again on the third day. Thinking about this from a psychological perspective, one might wonder what effect this would have on a person. I submit to you that one could simply not be able to stop talking about the things experienced while following Jesus.

---

[257]Though many are not; see Jn. 21:25.

What affect would witnessing such things have in a person's life today? It seems likely that the person who witnessed this in today's world would also not be able to stop talking about it. Even after spending twelve years in an insane asylum, one would still not be able to get witnessing miracles like this out of his or her mind. The reason is because it would be a life experience like no other; it would consume one's mind and would impact the observer with such force that he would not be able to keep such a thing to himself. An experience as such would transcend life itself in a sense. This is what happened with the Apostles of Christ. It seems that if *anyone* were alive at the time when Jesus' ministry was taking place, that people would not be able to keep in the things that they saw, even at the threat of death. If Jesus took anyone in and he saw the things that the apostles saw, he would be in the same predicament as the apostles; unable to stop talking about what he saw and experienced. The signs that Jesus did were so heavy for humanity that they are not only unforgotten today, but they are echoed through the generations and discussed every day of the week in every culture on Earth. This is not the case concerning the texts of Mormonism apart from the Bible.

Mormonism: Irrational (and Maximally Different from Christianity)

The Bible is true because the things mentioned in the Bible really happened.[258] They are historical events that took place, and we can read about them today. We can examine the evidence of these historical events archaeologically, philosophically, biblically, and rationally. It is not that there are no other truths in other texts comparatively, but the ultimate truth about life is found only in the Bible. It correctly and satisfyingly answers the questions: "How did we get here?"; "Why is there something rather than nothing?"; "How are we supposed to live?", and "What happens when we die?" Other so-called sacred texts

---

[258]See 1 Cor. 15:14.

are insufficient in explaining the answers to these questions because other so-called *sacred* texts, such as the *Doctrine and Covenants* are not ultimately true.

In Mormonism, one must believe that there is a multiverse, or more likely, that the universe itself existed forever in order to believe that Mormonism is true. The problem with this is that Mormonism teaches that when one dies, he has the chance to become a god of his own planet. This idea alone requires there to be an endless number of gods, as well as an endless number of planets in our solar system. For this teaching to work, that there are an endless number of planets or gods, then time would have to go backwards for an infinite amount of time, but this is impossible, because an infinite number of events (speaking of time itself), cannot come to an end, but it does come to an end in the event of today. Therefore, infinite regress is impossible because we arrive at *today*, but not yet *tomorrow*. In Mormonism, then, the teaching that there are an endless number of planets (because the god [*Heavenly Father*] Mormons believe that they now have, comes from or near a star called *Kolob*),[259] is consistent with their doctrine that "As man is, God once was, and as God is, man may become,"[260] but is philosophically impossible because it *requires* an infinite amount of time, which *tomorrow* itself proves that infinite regress does not conform to reality.

Based on the writings of Joseph Smith, then, we must conclude that he was either a deceiver (liar) or a lunatic because he never claimed to be Lord (as of his death).[261] On the contrary, when we look at the person of Jesus as described in the Bible, we see that not only did he perform

---

[259] Joseph Smith, *The Pearl of Great Price*, Abraham 3:16.

[260] Lorenzo Snow, *Teachings of the Presidents of the Church: Lorenzo Snow.* (Utah: Church of Jesus Christ of the Latter-day Saints. Intellectual Reserve, Incorporated. 2012), Chapter 5. https://www.churchofjesuschrist.org/study/manual/teachings-of-presidents-of-the-church-lorenzo-snow/chapter-5-the-grand-destiny-of-the-faithful?lang=eng.

[261] Anyone who makes such gigantic claims as Joseph Smith should probably be similarly examined through the principles of the trilemma of C. S. Lewis.

great miracles, make claims about himself that no human person in their right mind would claim, and rose from the dead. We find that he is true to his Word: He is the way, the truth, and the life.[262]

Christians should be careful in assuming what Mormons believe about Jesus. This is where apologetics comes in. One should remember to ask questions concerning the definitions of such words. This is one major focus in apologetics, discussing the definitions of certain words like, "Jesus," "Christian," "sin," and "salvation." For instance, someone could say, "Jesus is my Savior," but what one should know behind that claim is what is meant by the words "Jesus" and "savior." We have already discussed that even the Bible recognizes the false teachings of "another Jesus." Mormons describe something very different than what a Christian would describe. Mormon doctrine teaches that "Jesus" is the brother of Lucifer, the devil, and that he is not the one, true God. About the plan of salvation, Mormonism teaches that "it is by grace you are saved, after all you can do." There are extreme differences in the two comparisons here. In fact, they are in complete contradiction. The truth about reality then, cannot be both claims. The truth can only be one or the other, at best. Therefore, we should seek to not only know the truth, but how to articulate it and defend it.

Summary

Mormons try to argue that the Bible is corrupt, but it is not the Bible that is corrupt, but Joseph Smith. Since we can see that the Bible is true, we can know that all other religions are false, based on the fundamental law of non-contradiction. One is a Christian because Christianity is true, not because his parents are Christian or because he is American, but because Christianity is true. Something that helps us know that Christianity is true is the eyewitness accounts of the Apostles of Christ, and the archaeological evidence that corroborates the claims

---

[262]See Jn. 14:6.

as discussed in chapter five. We can know that Mormonism is irrational based on the assumptions concerning time and infinite sets. In the end, because we are so confident that Mormonism does not have any ground to stand on, we can offer our own challenge to Mormons based on the impossibility and yet the implications of the Law of the gods.

Chapter Seven:

Apologetics and Evangelism to Mormons

"But sanctify the Lord God in your hearts: and be ready always to give an answer to every man that asketh you a reason of the hope that is in you with meekness and fear." ~ 1 Peter 3:15

A GOOD STARTING point in developing and building a method for sharing the gospel to Mormons is that we *listen* to them.[263] Just as there are many people who call themselves Christians and do not yet know much about the Christian faith, there are also many who call themselves Mormons and do not know much of the Mormon faith.

Many Mormons consider themselves to be Christians, and not in the sense that "Mormons are Christians as well," but even further, several consider themselves to simply be another denomination of Evangelical Christianity. There is often a slight blend of worldviews, and on several levels. This, mixed with the idea that they can "feel" and know the truth by a "burning in the bosom"[264] leads a person to believe that there is a flair for the postmodern in the minds of several Mormons, including Joseph Smith, since he is the author of the *Doctrine and Covenants* and teaches such things within.

---

[263]Norman Geisler and David Geisler. *Conversational Evangelism* (Eugene: Harvest House Publishers), 2009.

[264]Joseph Smith, *Doctrine and Covenants*, 9:8.

My target in this methodological approach is specifically those with friends and family members in Mormonism, although when for instance, someone is at the barber shop or catching a ride on the subway and discovers that they are conversing with a Mormon while waiting, the following will still be beneficial. The bonus is that when one is talking with someone, whether it is a Mormon family member or not, he may never be able to predict which beliefs will come to the surface, but these principles cover a broad area in evangelism in a local context.

The Need for Apologetics

After beginning with, and developing the idea of listening, a following step should be discussing what postmodernism is and how it effects evangelism to Mormons and in general. One might explain what postmodernism is and perhaps use Nick Pollards explanation, which is basically that it means that the world no longer trusts in logic and in science to discover the truth, because it seems that the bursting of these things into modern culture did not really add much to anything. Modernity came from the age of enlightenment, and everyone thought that this new age would bring many answers to the questions people had. But the problem is that modernity did not seem to do that, so many are now *culturally* becoming postmodern, which seems, to most, the idea that there either is no truth or that everyone has their own truth.[265]

Complications in Mormon Thinking from Postmodernism

Some Mormons are postmodern in their thinking because this seems to be one way around problems introduced to them from their own scriptures. For instance, we have discussed Mormons presenting a person with the Moroni Challenge, "to feel within themselves" to see if the *Book of Mormon* is correct and true. Postmodernity teaches

---

[265]Nick Pollard. *Evangelism Made Slightly Less Difficult: how to interest people who aren't interested* (Downers Grove: InterVarsity Press), 1997.

that whatever is true for a specific person might be different for another person. But the problem with this is that one cannot test the truth of certain claims because they often begin as untrue and irrational. They are frequently inconsistent and self-refuting. For instance, if someone were to say, "Yes, Christianity is true, and so is Mormonism,"[266] they would be engaging in a contradiction as mentioned above, and therefore be in violation of a fundamental logical law. If something is true for one person then it is true for that person and everyone else. For instance, if Reginald feels cold living in Alaska, then it is also true for Jasper, living in England, that Reginald feels cold, even if it is a hot summer day in England. The truth is in the object, not the subject. This is one great confusion concerning truth in modern times.[267]

William Lane Craig says, "In my opinion this sort of thinking could not be more mistaken. The idea that we live in a postmodern culture is a myth. ... Nobody is a postmodernist when it comes to reading the labels on a medicine bottle verses a box of rat poison."[268] The point is clear: No one *actually* lives as if relativism were true. This continues to hammer down the idea that truth is not only knowable but is also discernable from what is not true. Because we can discern the truth, we can know beyond a reasonable doubt which, if any, religions are ultimately true.

What is unfortunate is that even from within the Christian community, people claim that there are so many Christian Bible interpretations that we cannot possibly know which one is true, then proceed to write them *all* off. Many people believe that because the *Book of Mormon* is a sacred text, and because the *Bhagavad-Gita* is a sacred text, and because the *Necronomicon* is a sacred text, they know that

---

[266]This is akin to saying that Mormons are also Christians, or that they also worship Jesus.

[267]Again, how is the Moroni Challenge any different than if one were to ask it of the Quran?

[268]William Lane Craig, *Reasonable Faith: Christin truth and apologetics* (Wheaton: Crossway, 2008), 18.

all of these are mostly comprised of illogical and unfounded gibberish. Then, because the Bible is also a sacred text, it must also be comprised of gibberish. This is an erroneous conclusion.

The major problem here is not only that these types of claims come from ignorance but that they employ the fallacy of association. This is in the hasty generalization family, which assumes the same truth for a group of things that are in a similar category somehow. "It confuses typical and atypical evidence, or ignores atypical evidence entirely, then jumps to a conclusion. It concludes too much from too little, choosing only the evidence it wants."[269] On the other hand, if someone is making the claim that the *Joseph Smith Translation* of the Bible is equal in holiness, truth claims, or in being sacred as the *King James Version* or other popular evangelical translations of the Bible, then they are associating the Christian Bible with a translation that is a calamitously inaccurate translation of the Koine Greek New Testament and the Hebrew and Aramaic Old Testament. This would also conclude too much from too little. Just because all these other so-called sacred writings are found fallacious, does not mean that *all* sacred writings are fallacious.

It seems that this fallacy is on the rise *because* of postmodernism. From an atheistic perspective, this might seem like a good argument at first (that all sacred books are erroneous, therefore none of them are true), but as people bring their presuppositions to the table before examining the text, they fall short in the long run and are in error from the beginning of their argument. Fortunately, people can learn to see that it is possible to discern the truth and examine these texts one by one and discover which of them they should continue to examine.

It seems wise at this point to discuss *pre-evangelism,* that is, the idea that we need to till the soil of the mind before we plant the seed of the gospel (soil tilling is sometimes required to help people understand

---

[269]Norman L. Geisler and Ronald M. Brooks, *Come, Let Us Reason: An introduction to logical thinking* (Grand Rapids, 1990), 105.

the need for soil tilling).[270] In other words, there may be some things we need to do before we share the gospel because the heart is not always ready to hear the gospel. This is why there is such a need for pre-evangelism. Because postmodernism has caused the world to churn into a muck and mire of confusion and disarray.

Mature Christians must be careful about expecting others (Mormons, homosexuals, juvenile Christians, etc.) to think and act like mature Christians. Some Christians tend to believe that everyone else should believe and think exactly as they do, but the fact is that no two people have all the same presuppositions. The reason for this is because no two people have all the exact same experiences. This is why Christians must also be careful about when we hear someone say that he is a Christian, that he might not mean the same thing that we do, such as with a Mormon.

We need to keep in mind that some Christians are drinking milk while others are eating meat.[271] We cannot expect Christians to all be as spiritually mature as everyone else, and believers cannot expect non-believers to act like a Christian. When a person claims to be a Christian, it seems fitting to have the question in mind, *What do they think they know about Jesus?* Even Mormons themselves say, "I am a Christian," yet they often really know little of Jesus of Nazareth.

Expecting Mormons and non-believers to think and act like mature Christians hinders their growth because we are not making right judgments about them, and it often is revealed in our body language towards them, as well as in our tone. The basic idea here is to say that Christians should not assume what people know, regardless of what *camps* they believe that a person adheres to, whether that is Mormonism or anything. We need to make right judgments about people.[272] A good way to do this is by asking simple questions. Through

---

[270]Geisler and Geisler, *Conversational Evangelism*, 25.

[271]See Heb. 5:12–14.

[272]See Jn. 7:24.

asking simple questions, I once discovered in a conversation that a Mormon whom I was speaking with, also *equally* considered himself to be a Muslim (speaking of postmodernism). Perhaps this is needless to say, but the soil needed to be thoroughly tilled before we were even able to begin to discuss the gospel.

Major Worldviews

Many fallacious worldviews are strongly adhered to because of the influence of postmodernism. The idea is that everyone can have his own truth, but the major problem is that many of these worldviews completely contradict one another at their most fundamental teachings. It seems prudent at this point that we should briefly take a transcendent look at some worldviews so the reader can understand where Mormons are coming from better. A worldview is simply the way a person views the world. What consequences does this have though? It is why we make the decisions that we do, it is why we believe what we do, and it is why we behave the way we do. For instance, if one were famously arguing, "But, we have never done it that way before!" while the way they were doing "it" was neither beneficial nor successful to or for anyone, it is likely because of the way they view the world through their own presuppositions. This is why it is good to recognize presuppositions. For another example, at dinnertime, one might wash his hands in an eccentric manner before he eats, simply because there are unfounded beliefs about a purity ritual that he has subconsciously developed over time. One might refrain from watching horror movies because he believes it is a bad omen from poor interpretations from his past experiences. These are *presuppositions*, and they are a part of our worldview; the way we view the world. The main problem with presuppositions is that they can be false.

In any event, there are several worldviews to briefly consider: *Theism*: Miracles are possible. *Deism*: Miracles are not possible. *Atheism*: God does not exist. *Polytheism*: Many gods exist and are worshiped. *Pantheism*: God is identified with the world. *Panentheism*: God is in everything and growing with the world. *Finite godism*: God is *finite* in power and perfection. *Agnosticism*: Not knowing if God exists (which is basically atheism by many standards today).[273] *Henotheism/ monolatry*: (This is Mormonism) The belief that many gods exist, but only worshiping and focusing on one deity (i.e. Heavenly Father).

An important idea to emphasize is that a person should not *ask* another what worldview he is, but this is something that a Christian should *discover* by investigation through conversation. If we ask someone what worldview he is, we will likely run into some strange looks or people who assume the wrong definition of a worldview, followed by an answer that does not follow. The idea here again is to *listen to them*. The reason we should do this is so that we can be more prepared when tilling the soil of one's mind.

Easier Conversations

Often, when we engage in conversations, we might forget that *we get in our own way*, so to speak. We get fired up because we know that what the person is saying is very wrong and not biblical, and as apologists, we just want to fight against that with everything we have, but what happens is that we often end up building walls against trust. It is good to continuously remind oneself that the goal is to win the person over, not simply win an argument.

At the same time, we want to locate presuppositions and ask questions which show the person where they are speaking in a manner that does not follow. For instance, when a Mormon says that people can become gods, we could ask the question how this is possible since we have been born (how does eternity to eternity fit in this?); we have sinned (how can God sin?), and we die. What Mormons are essentially saying is that the god that they now have was a sinner in the past, when

---

[273]Adapted from Norman L. Geisler and Ronald M. Brooks. *When Skeptics Ask: A handbook on Christian evidences.* (Grand Rapids: Baker Books, 2013), 30.

he was a man. So, then our best way to reveal these fallacious ways of thinking is by asking questions that cause them to think about what they are truly saying. Many times, one becomes a Mormon when they are young, before they learn to question things. Then the Latter-day Saint church just becomes the law, and they become afraid to question anything. This is why it seems that in many cases, when a person leaves Mormonism, it is because they were confronted with a question that they could not answer and just could not move past. This is why it is good to ask the question, "Why do men become gods?" This can help a Mormon think and dwell on something until something snaps, like the "straw that broke the camel's back," so to speak.

A good question to ask oneself and continue this discussion would be along the lines of, "What kind of barriers are there that people have that keep them from coming to Jesus?" We want to know what keeps a person from receiving the gospel. It seems that there may be only three different barriers to the gospel. In other words, there are three kinds of doubts when it comes to believing the gospel, no matter what someone believes beforehand. These barriers are *emotional barriers, intellectual barriers, and volitional barriers.*[274] Normally, *volitional barriers* are likely the strongest of barriers as well as most common, but in the case of Mormonism, it seems that the barriers are *primarily intellectual and emotional.* The reason there are emotional barriers is because they are tied (or chained) to Mormonism already, because if they leave the faith, then they will be excommunicated, and treated poorly by all who they know and love.

There is a great societal incentive for Mormons to remain Mormon. Another example of an emotional barrier would be when someone says that "There is so much evil in the world." They cannot believe in God because their child had died, or their parent abused them, or something of that nature. The problem is that none of these objections make the

---

[274]D. A. Carson, Ed., *Telling the Truth: Evangelizing Postmoderns* (Grand Rapids: Zondervan, 2000), 280–286.

existence of God impossible. None of these objections are influenced by the truth.

An example of an intellectual barrier could be "I don't believe in God because of evolution, naturalism, or a specific cosmological model other than the standard, etc." Just because someone does not believe that God exists, does not mean that he does not exist. Often people believe that they have intellectual reservations about believing in God. These are usually overcome with arguments and evidence for God. Some will say that a person cannot be argued into the kingdom of heaven, but this does not mean that the Holy Spirit cannot use arguments and evidence in order to soften the heart of someone to receive the gospel. Mormons generally have an intellectual barrier based on their assumptions of the Mormon Jesus and the biblical Jesus being the same Jesus, and the idea that the Bible has been corrupted (yet ironically does not disagree with Mormon theology).

An example of a volitional barrier comes from the will, or desire of a person. It might sound like, "I don't want there to be a God because then I'll have to answer to Him. I want to live the way I want to live!" Perhaps he is addicted to something that hinders him from seeing the truth about God and is afraid of having to let it go.

The problem with these barriers is that they do not argue against what is true. In speaking of intellectual barriers, there are powerful arguments for the existence of God, which we have already discussed. In speaking of emotional barriers, just because God allowed a tsunami to happen, which resulted in killing one's grandmother in a tragic death does not mean that God does not exist. I discuss this because I want the readers to have at least some understanding of how these barriers work.

In Mormonism, it seems that the intellectual and emotional barriers are more prevalent because Mormons already believe in a form of theism. In any case, we should try to locate the barriers that people put up against the gospel because these help us to see *where* to focus a lot of our energy in the discussion. For instance, if a Mormon says that they believe that the *Book of Mormon* is true over the Bible because of a feeling they had, we can show them that the feeling is not good evidence for what is true because then it is our feelings (emotional barrier) that become our guiding factor for truth, but we all seem to resonate with knowing that the heart is deceitful above all else.[275] So there must be a better standard in addition to the heart for discovering the truth, such as with understanding the fundamental laws of logic paired with scripture.

Classical Apologetics Is Useful for Witnessing to Mormons

We can use the discussion on the barriers to the gospel as the spring-board for a discussion on the classical apologetics model. Classical apologetics is the method of apologetics that begins with the idea that truth is knowable. Then moves to arguments for the existence of God, which Mormons already believe in (in a polluted manner), even if they do not yet understand that they believe in a transcendent Supreme Being, which we can reveal to them through the Mormon Cosmological Argument for the Existence of One Supreme God. Finally, we move to the veracity of the Bible and the truth about Christ and the state of mankind. This is my personal method of classical apologetics for Mormons.

We Can Know the Truth through the Fundamental Laws of Logic

This should be the first step in the classical apologetics approach, that the truth can be known. We have the capacity to think for ourselves, at least on some level. We have already discussed these laws at length, so we will only touch on them here. The first law is the law of identity, which is the idea that whatever something is, that is what it is. We need to be able to identify one thing from another. In other words, Jim is Jim. Jim is not Bob. It is so simple, in fact, that one does not normally ever really think much about it.

---

[275]See Jer. 17:9.

The second law is the law of non-contradiction. This means that when a claim is made, that claim cannot be both true and false at the same time and in the same sense. For instance, if someone were to say that "Woman X is pregnant," then it could not be the case that she is not pregnant if it were true that she was pregnant. Similarly, if Woman X made the claim that she is not pregnant, if there were, in fact, no babies growing in her womb, then it could not be true that she is pregnant. A claim cannot be both true and false at the same time and in the same sense.

Finally, we come to the law of excluded middle. This law says that every claim is either true *or* false. There are no other alternatives. Either the claim that "Woman X is pregnant" is true *or* it is false. Likewise, either the claim that "Woman X is not pregnant," is true or it is false. To use another example, the light is either on or off. There are no other options.

Through these laws, we can know what is true and what is false. In other words, the truth can be known through these three laws of logic. In speaking with Mormons, these laws can be used in the same way. If something is contradicting, as for instance, 2 Nephi 25:23 and Ephesians 2:8-9, the law of non-contradiction shows us that both cannot be true. Neither one *must* be true based on logic, but they cannot both be true because they contradict one another. We should also measure the historical claims of the Book of Mormon for instance, with this same way of thinking.

Heavenly Father Falls Short of the Glory of God

The first step was to show that the truth can be known. The next step in this approach is to show that the One Supreme God exists through the Mormon Cosmological Argument for the Existence of One Supreme God, ultimately the Christian God. Here, we should argue through the principle of causality (every effect has a cause) that there must be an ultimate beginning and that infinite regress is impossible. But remember, we should discuss this with gentleness and respect.[276]

From here, we can move to a direct discussion on **The Mormon Cosmological Argument for the Existence of One Supreme God** once the principle of causality and the Law of the gods is nailed down:

1. If the Law of the gods transcends the gods (Heavenly Fathers) in Mormonism, then there is one Supreme God who wrote the Law or caused its existence.
2. The Law of the gods transcends all Heavenly Fathers.
3. Therefore, there is one Supreme God, who is the author of the Law.

Christians can use this argument to show that the reality about God cannot possibly work the way Mormonism teaches, and we are going in this direction with the Mormon Cosmological Argument because we need to also show that *a transcendent being is required for any Heavenly Father at all to exist.* Mormons do not typically believe in a transcendent being *in the sense that there is a being that transcends all Heavenly Fathers.* In other words, *we need to demonstrate to them through the Mormon Cosmological Argument that a being exists which transcends all Heavenly Fathers.* This is possible and probable because there is a being that transcends the universe, understood namely through the Kalam Cosmological Argument. Remember that clarification and accurate definitions from person to person are always a top priority in such discussions. At this step, it is also good to keep on pressing the principle of causality, because we want to plant seeds of doubt at minimum. If a Mormon dances around the idea or says that you do not understand the nature of godhood in Latter-day Saint theology, then simply tell them that you want to know why the pattern of exaltation came about in the first place. If we go through exaltation like Heavenly

---

[276]See 1 Pet. 3:15.

Father, then it was clearly not Heavenly Father that instituted exaltation in the first place, but Heavenly Father came under the exaltation that was already in place. This will help them understand where you are coming from. If Heavenly Father is *as we are now*, then he would have been in the same boat, so to speak, otherwise they must admit that their official doctrines and scriptures are mistaken, and Heavenly Father was not *as we are now*.

The Bible Is True and Uncorrupted

After the second step is thoroughly discussed, we move on to the third and final step, which is that the Bible is true, and what it says about Jesus, salvation, and the state of man is true. The reason we discuss this is because Mormons tend to believe that the Bible is corrupted, and that the *Book of Mormon* is "the most correct book of any that are on planet earth."[277] Mormons frequently tend to believe that a scribe has traced over the letters of the biblical "manuscript" as the letters have faded through time, and the scribes who traced over this could have manipulated the biblical text, being influenced by the devil, or the like, and changed the words of the Holy Bible. In any event, what we want to show here is that the Bible has not been corrupted, and that the scriptures that we have today are accurate which we can know through seeing the many copies of handwritten manuscripts that are currently in libraries and museums all over the world side-by-side, so to speak, as extensively discussed in the beginning of chapter six. So, then we can know that the things that are spoken about Jesus and by Jesus are true and precise. When a Mormon understands that the Bible has not been corrupted, then he or she can know that because the Bible and the *Book of Mormon* positively contradict one another (which is a major part of the goal, to show that they do in fact contradict one another), and that because of such, only one of them can be true. The Bible has not only

---

[277]This again falls right in line with what Muslims believe about the Quran.

strong archaeological evidence to attest to its truth, *whereas the Book of Mormon does not even have a shred of archaeological evidence*, but the events in the Bible are also attested *extra-biblically*.[278] Sources outside the Bible attest to the accuracy of what is found in the Bible.

There Is More than One Box

As in every religion, not all Mormons fit in the same box, so to speak. The reason this is the case is because there are a lot of words that are misused, and not always on purpose. That said, Christians sometimes use our own language as well. Some people call it *Christianese*, which is basically using words like, *sin, Bible, Christian, saved, sanctification, Jesus*, and such. Now what is problematic here is that when we say the name, Jesus, to a Mormon, they believe that we are saying the word with the same meaning that they believe the word Jesus means. The Mormon Jesus is different than the biblical Jesus (Hopefully, this is obvious by now!).[279] So, when we are talking with a Mormon, it is good to discover what they mean when they say these words. As discussed above, there are sometimes people who attend both Christian churches and Mormon *wards* (which are often referred to even by Mormons as *churches*). So, there is not even a difference with the word *church* in a lot of people's minds. Many think that they are all the same, whether Mormon or not. This is why we need to understand what a person believes when discussing who the real Jesus is, and what true, biblical Christianity looks like. After discovering where a person comes from, we need to ask questions in a way that causes him to question why he believes what he does.

---

[278]For ten examples, see Brian Windle, *Top Ten Historical References to Jesus Outside of the Bible*, Bible Archaeology Report: November, 2022. https://biblearchaeologyreport.com/2022/11/18/top-ten-historical-references-to-jesus-outside-of-the-bible/.

[279]See 2 Cor. 11:4.

Challenging the Challenge and Planting More Seeds of Doubt

In Matthew chapter twenty-one, verses twenty-three through twenty-seven, Jesus is confronted by the chief priests and the elders of the people and presented to him a question. What is interesting is how he answered this question.

> And when he was come into the temple, the chief priests and the elders of the people came unto him as he was teaching, and said, By what authority doest thou these things? and who gave thee this authority? And Jesus answered and said unto them, I also will ask you one thing, which if ye tell me, I in like wise will tell you by what authority I do these things. The baptism of John, whence was it? from heaven, or of men? And they reasoned with themselves, saying, If we shall say, From heaven; he will say unto us, Why did ye not then believe him? But if we shall say, Of men; we fear the people; for all hold John as a prophet. And they answered Jesus, and said, We cannot tell. And he said unto them, Neither tell I you by what authority I do these things.'[280]

It seems that one could very likely use this same principle in witnessing to Mormons, with the hope of having them further investigate their own doctrine. Jesus, in the citation above made a bargain with them. He said that if they can tell Him this one specific thing that He would tell them what they wanted to know. Similarly, when confronted by a Mormon with the Moroni challenge, or about joining his church, or reading the *Book of Mormon*, a person could say, "I'll consider coming to your church or reading the *Book of Mormon* if you can satisfyingly tell me one thing, *why* do men become gods?" The thing is,

---

[280]Mt. 21:23–27.

that perhaps they will do what is typically done when they are asked this question, which is that they will say something along the lines of, "Heavenly Father loving his children." But this is not to what one is referring. Make it clear before making any promises, but this will help motivate them to investigate the Law of the gods, and while they are looking, they will never be able come up with an answer. The fact which will stare at them square in the face is that they must believe the doctrine of exaltation not only against that which is logical, but they must admit that a blind faith is a requirement for the church of Jesus Christ of the Latter-day saints, which is really no faith at all. On the contrary, biblical Christianity is evidence-based faith.

We plant seeds of doubt in their minds when we ask well thought out questions. It seems that a good place to begin raising doubt is to ask a question like, "What is it that makes you believe what you do about Mormonism?" Or "How did you become LDS, and what is it that makes you remain as such?" These questions will hopefully lead the conversation into a discussion about the *Book of Mormon*. Often, a Mormon will talk about how he felt something, and you will discover that his knowledge is based on how he feels. On the other hand, a person could continue with explaining the idea that the Bible is constantly and consistently attested historically and archaeologically, and that it is fascinating how deep it gets. Remember that Mormons claim that the Bible is one of their own sacred texts as well. We could say something like, "It strengthens my faith knowing that I can look at the Bible and see, through reason and evidence, that the Bible is true."

In the book, *Sharing the Gospel with Mormons*, Eric Johnson also presents an excellent question for planting seeds of doubt: "Why do you think that God would do this with the Bible and not with the *Book of Mormon?*"[281] Why would God make the Bible corroborated through reason and evidence but not the *Book of Mormon*? It seems that by asking a question like this, a Mormon should have doubts about their

---

[281]Eric Johnson and Sean McDowell. *Sharing the Good News with Mormons* (Eugene: Harvest House Publishers, 2018), 180.

sacred text and hopefully will help them want to talk about the Bible further. The goal here is to have our focus on the texts rather than on the persons in the conversation. We want to look at this together, in a sense. This leads us to the next idea.

Gentleness and Respect

We want them to feel like they are on a journey *with us*. We do not always want to trap people in their contradictions and inconsistencies, because this is often when people want to run in the opposite direction. For instance, when we discuss the clear contradiction between the *Book of Mormon* and the Bible, we can ask them in a gentle manner how they put these two things together in their minds. How do we become saved, "After all we can do," the way the *Book of Mormon* describes, and "by the gift of God, not by works," the way that the Bible describes? One text says that salvation comes through what we can do, and the other says that salvation comes by nothing we can do but as a gift. "How is this reconciled?" From asking these gentle questions we are building a strong case for the truth of the Bible without being abrasive, which often causes defensiveness.

Keep the Conversation Going

When we ask a Mormon why they trust the *Book of Mormon* and, in comparison to the Bible, we ask him or her why God would provide evidence and reason for the veracity of the Bible and not the *Book of Mormon*, we invite further discussion. When the Mormon is left feeling like he or she has a taste of hopelessness, then we can share the hope of Jesus in our own lives. We can tell Mormons that we as Christians are filled with hope and it gives us a great peace, because Jesus is enough. We do not need the janitor who sweeps up our mess behind us in order to make us righteous. We need the real Jesus. The whole Jesus. Just like the fact that we cannot pick ourselves up by our own bootstraps, he alone makes us righteous. We have no part in our own righteousness. This is why we are so in love with Jesus. Because he first loved us. Salvation is a free gift, and what part of a gift can be earned?

I think a simple question that should also be asked of our Mormon friends concerning the *burning in the bosom* is, "Do your feelings differ from day to day? How about what you crave? One day we want apple pie and the next day we don't want anything to do with apple pie, and instead we want a salad or a steak. How can we base something as important as our spiritual journey on the way we feel when we can't even trust that our feelings are stable with what we eat?" *Our hearts change like the wind.* Why would we place so much trust in what we feel? When we are teenagers in the dating scene, one day we are *in love* with a girl and one day we are *in love* with a completely different girl. Jeremiah chapter seventeen, verse nine, teaches us that the heart is deceitful above all things.[282] Proverbs chapter four, verse twenty-three, explains that above everything else, we should guard our hearts.[283] These verses are saying the same thing, *that the human heart is extremely vulnerable.* These verses are saying that the heart of a person is something that requires a lot of attention because of how desperate and quick it is to move or to be moved. So how can we protect our hearts?

This is the type of question that will hopefully leave them desiring to hear more. Since Mormons base the foundation of their faith on their feelings, we can confront the idea of the stability of our feelings with the truth of the Bible and the experiences of life in general. Mormons will likely recognize these feelings being unstable in a minute moment of introspection.

We protect our hearts with our minds.[284] We protect the way we feel with intellect. Similarly, when we feel a burning in our bosom, this

---

[282]See Jer. 17:9.

[283]See Prov. 4:23.

[284]See 2 Cor. 10:5.

does not mean that something is true. When we feel love for someone, it does not mean that this person is the best person for us. We often discover this through hindsight. We guard our hearts with our minds. It is curious that a Muslim can feel a burning in the bosom about the Quran, just like someone can feel a burning in the bosom about what the *Book of Mormon* says. Which one is true though? If these things are different, and oppose one another, how is it that we can know which religion is true?

Our hearts lead us into all kinds of trouble. This is one reason why there are so many single mothers in our world today. How is it that we can put so much trust in the way we feel? Why is it that some Latter-day Saints have had a burning in the bosom and then left their faith and came to biblical Christianity? Is it because their feelings have changed? Or is it because of something else?

Some Considerations

What types of risks should we be willing to take? I remember in eighth grade, my health teacher, Mrs. Morrison, was discussing the idea that we take risks even by getting out of bed in the morning. We drive to school or work, and we put faith in the painted yellow lines on the road that will keep us safe from harm. We risk our lives at some level or another every day.

As Christians, we all have friends and relatives who are of a different belief system than our own. We might be cousins, neighbors, friends, or siblings with a Mormon, and often we are very close to him. We love him; we care for him, and we think about his concept of reality and truth. At the same time, we know that Jesus is the way, the truth, and the life and that no one comes to the Father but through Him,[285] and that they do not have the real, biblical Jesus.[286]

---

[285]See Jn. 14:6.

[286]See 1 Jn. 5:11–12.

The thought of this can be saddening, angering, and even terrifying. This is something we must think about if we really care for Mormons. What is more important, that we go through life as if nothing is wrong, or that we have serious discussions about what happens when we die with our loved ones? Is it better that we have a fun relationship with them now and they end up leaving earth not knowing who Jesus of Nazareth is, or that they don't like us as much in the beginning of our agenda to introduce them to Jesus and they end up in eternity with us and with the King of kings and Lord of lords?

Paul says in Romans chapter nine, verses one through five,

> I say the truth in Christ, I lie not, my conscience also bearing me witness in the Holy Ghost, That I have great heaviness and continual sorrow in my heart. For I could wish that myself were accursed from Christ for my brethren, my kinsmen according to the flesh: Who are Israelites; to whom pertaineth the adoption, and the glory, and the covenants, and the giving of the law, and the service of God, and the promises; Whose are the fathers, and of whom as concerning the flesh Christ came, who is over all, God blessed for ever. Amen.[287]

Paul seems to agree that his friends and family are a priority over even himself. He was willing to stay out of heaven if it meant that his fellow Israelites were able to know and trust in Jesus. He was deeply saddened for good reason, as we should also be for our friends and relatives who do not know the King of kings.

Consider this for a moment. The Bible tells believers to "Contend for the faith."[288] Does this exclude those who are close to us? Certainly

---

[287]Ro. 9:1–5.

[288]See Jude, verse 3.

not. God is patient with us and desires that none should perish![289] It seems that if they are close to us, we should be able to discuss the things of eternal life with them with more frequency, especially if we know that they are lost. The fact that we have loved ones who are heading to hell for eternity should, through our love, sadness, anger, and terror, motivate us to talk with them about Jesus and where they will spend eternity. Use your relationships for the glory of God.

People seem to avoid or prevent talking to their friends and loved ones about Jesus perhaps because they do not see an immediate urgency to share Jesus. They might live in the moment. People who live in the moment are not thinking about their future. They are not seeing that they exist for eternity. Colossians chapter three, verses one and two says, "If ye then be risen with Christ, seek those things which are above, where Christ sitteth on the right hand of God. Set your affection on things above, not on things on the earth."[290] Did you catch that? "Seek those things which are above...." In other words, think about the things which are eternal and permanent (namely, Christ). This life on earth is temporary, and if we see our lives as even semi-permanent, we will not see the need to be urgent in sharing Jesus with unbelievers. It is worth the risk in speaking with friends and family members about the truth of Christianity and the false hope of Mormonism.

This is one reason one studies apologetics. Apologetics helps us know the answers when we are confronted with tough questions concerning faith and theology. Apologetics gives us confidence in sharing our faith. We need all we can get! Think about it, are you going to want to engage in conversations that you know nothing about? Apologetics helps a person conquer his or her own fears in sharing the gospel. Moreover, apologetics is truth seeking. If Mormonism *were* the one true religion, then we should be Mormons. The fact is, Christianity is true, and therefore we are Christians.

---

[289]See 2 Pet. 3:9.

[290]Col. 3:1–2.

Talk with your friends, your family members, your neighbors about the Good News of Jesus Christ. We are commissioned by him to do this.[291] Paul even reasons in Romans chapter ten, verses fourteen and fifteen, "How then shall they call on him in whom they have not believed? and how shall they believe in him of whom they have not heard? and how shall they hear without a preacher? And how shall they preach, except they be sent? as it is written, How beautiful are the feet of them that preach the gospel of peace, and bring glad tidings of good things!"[292]

The Roman Road

When we have journeyed through the steps in the classical apologetics method, we should now use discretion on leading a person to the foot of the cross. The Roman Road is simple, but solid, just like the ancient roads in Rome. This is something that you can easily share with all people in order to lead them to Christ. Depending on who you speak with, the Roman Road could have several verses included in it. The Roman Road is called such because one leads another to Christ through different verses in the book of Romans. I like to use four verses from Romans because this makes it easier to remember, and it seems to take out further complicated thoughts. First, Romans 3:23 says that we all fall short of the glory of God. This means that we do not meet the standard that God is. He is the standard of goodness, and we fail to meet him as the standard in our goodness. The proof for this comes from an honest analysis of the Ten Commandments, but all you really need to look at is simply one of them. Think about the Seventh Commandment for example, that "Thou shalt not commit adultery."[293] Jesus clarifies this commandment in the sermon on the mount in Matthew chapter five.

---

[291]See the Great Commission, Mt. 28:19.

[292]Ro. 10:14–15.

[293]Ex. 20:14.

He says that "That whosoever looketh on a woman to lust after her hath committed adultery with her already in his heart."[294] I think that not only does this show how disastrously far we are from the standard of goodness that is God, but I think that through it, Jesus is saying, "See how desperately you need me." We fall short of God's glory.

Second, in the Roman Road, we turn to Romans 6:23, which says "For the wages of sin is death; but the gift of God is eternal life through Jesus Christ our Lord." This is to say that the cost of our sin (our moral failures against God), is the reason why we die. The death rate is 1/1. Ten out of ten people die. The reason why we die is because we have sinned. But this is not the end of the verse. Paul says, "but the gift of God is eternal life through Christ Jesus our Lord." In other words, death is a temporary setback to our existence. We will live for eternity.

Third, in Romans 5:8, we read, "God shows his love for us in that while we were still sinners, Christ died for us." So, in the middle of the act of our sin, he did the biggest act of love possible: He died for us. He took our place on the cross. This shows us that God loves us. This verse also helps answer why God would do such a thing as giving us a gift of eternal life and saving us from judgment.

Similarly, John 3:16 says that "For God so loved the world, that he gave his only begotten Son, that whosoever believeth in him should not perish, but have everlasting life." God loves you so much that he himself became a man in the body of Jesus Christ and came to earth to die for our sins (See John 1:14). This is essential for a person to understand that God loves him or her. It is essential because he or she can have a personal relationship with him, which is what he wants. He communicated to us in human language, the message of the Bible. The historical events that actually took place in the Bible are written down so that all may learn about and know him.

Fourth, God loves all people unconditionally, but there is a condition for salvation. The condition is found in our final verse in the

---

[294]Mt. 5:28.

Roman Road: Romans 10:9. It reads, "That if thou shalt confess with thy mouth the Lord Jesus, and shalt believe in thine heart that God hath raised him from the dead, thou shalt be saved." Confess with your physical mouth that Jesus is Lord, because professing your faith and sharing your faith is infinitely important to one's Christian journey.[295]

Believe in your heart that God raised Him from the dead, because Christianity is based on a historical fact. Then you will be saved. This verse, Romans 10:9, is a *Modus Ponens* syllogism. What that means is that it is essentially an "if, then" argument. IF you confess and believe, THEN you will be saved. This is the condition for salvation, which is not much of condition at all. One does not burn any extra calories in believing in and trusting in Jesus for their eternal destination. "For by grace are ye saved through faith; and that not of yourselves: it is the gift of God: Not of works, lest any man should boast."[296] We cannot earn a gift, any more than we can earn forgiveness.

Remember that when you are trying to share the gospel that the gift of salvation is for everyone to receive, but only some will take the free gift. Don't beat yourself up about what you could have, should have, or would have said, because ultimately it is not you who works on the heart of a person, but this is the work of the Spirit (see John 16:8). In any event, there is no question that He can use you to bring someone into the Kingdom of God (see Romans 10:14-15). The Roman Road is where one's relationship with Jesus **begins**, not ends. From here, encourage Bible reading, sound Church attendance, and prayer. In any case, encourage **remaining** in the Vine.[297]

---

[295]See Matthew 10:32–33.

[296]Eph. 2:8–9.

[297]See John 15.

Summary

Asking *why* people can become gods will likely cause a Mormon to have raised doubts. This question will also hopefully create an eventual desire to hear more about the truth of the Bible. To summarize everything discussed and to continue looking at this Mormon doctrine from every angle possible, the following is again, from the Latter-day Saint website:

What is Exaltation?

> Exaltation is eternal life, the kind of life God lives. He lives in great glory. He is perfect. He possesses all knowledge and all wisdom. He is the Father of spirit children. He is a creator. We can become like our Heavenly Father. This is Exaltation.
>
> If we prove faithful to the Lord, we will live in the highest degree of the celestial kingdom of heaven. We will become exalted, to live with our Heavenly Father in eternal families. Exaltation is the greatest gift that Heavenly Father can give His children.[298]

We discussed this in part in chapter two, and we discovered that their scriptures teach that when a Mormon man dies, that if he were: 1) good enough, 2) if he were married, and 3) if he followed the "law," that he would become *exalted*.

Doctrine and Covenants has been our main focus. In verse nineteen of section one hundred and thirty-two, the *Doctrine and Covenants* teaches that if a man marries a wife, and if he "abides in my covenant ... they shall pass by the angels, and the gods, which are set there (in eternity), to their Exaltation and glory in all things, as hath been

---

[298]The Church of Jesus Crist of the Latter-Day Saints. *Exaltation*. https://www.churchofjesuschrist.org/study/manual/gospel-principles/chapter-47-Exaltation?lang=eng.

sealed upon their heads...."[299] and continuing immediately in verse twenty we read, "Then shall they be gods"[300] (which verse twenty actually says this twice, as if there were any questions about it).

In verse twenty-nine, "Abraham received all things ... and hath entered into his Exaltation and sitteth upon his throne."[301] Continuing to verse thirty-seven: "Abraham received concubines, and they bore him children; and it was accounted unto him for righteousness ... and because they did none other things than which they were commanded, they have entered into their Exaltation, according to the promises, and sit upon thrones, and are not angels but are gods."[302]

It is clear both in this section of *Doctrine and Covenants* as well as in several other pieces of literature found in the Latter-day Saint movement that their core doctrines teach that when a man dies, he becomes the god of his own world, populating that planet. After all, "As man is, God once was, and as God now is, man may become."

So here again is the problem. If Heavenly Father was once like us, then that means that there were other men on the same planet he came from who rules other worlds (e. g. his parents). If Heavenly Father were alone on that planet, then he could not become a god, because the *Doctrine and Covenants* tells us that a requirement for becoming a god is that he must have a wife. So, as we have discussed, there was at least one other woman in this world from which he came. We can assume that they had children and populated that planet as well. But it is also safe to assume that there were other couples on that planet as well. For instance, where did his wife come from? Where did he come from? One can clearly see that this planet that God (as we supposedly now know him) lived on was populated indefinitely. The significance

---

[299] Joseph Smith. *Doctrine and Covenants,* 132:19–20.

[300] Ibid.

[301] Ibid. 132:29.

[302] Ibid.

here is that Mormon doctrine unquestionably requires an infinite past, and that there are an infinite number of men who became gods.

It is the same with time. For the doctrine of gods in Mormonism to be logically consistent, there must be an infinite amount of time in the past, because according to Mormon scriptures, there is no sole, powerful, creator who made the universe in which we live. According to Mormonism, the universe always existed,[303] and these gods are basically reduced to alien-humans who were good enough to become gods from other planets. But there are several issues with this. One is that an infinite amount of time cannot exist, since we haven't yet experienced tomorrow, but yesterday we have, and we know that tomorrow is going to happen, Lord willing, which will be the moment in the space-time continuum where time itself is bound. In order for an infinite amount of time to exist, it would have to be a *complete set* of time, which tomorrow proves that an infinite amount of time is not a complete set, and therefore, not reality. Therefore, *infinite regress* is impossible because we arrive at *today*, but not yet *tomorrow*. In Mormonism, then, the teaching that there are an endless number of planets (because the god [Heavenly Father] Mormons believe that they now have, comes from, or near, a star called Kolob), which lines up with their doctrine that "As man is, God once was, and as God is, man may become," is philosophically impossible because it requires an infinite amount of time, which *tomorrow* itself proves that infinite regress does not correspond to reality.

Since Joseph Smith teaches that Heavenly Father populated a planet with billions of people who have the potential to become gods of their own planets and do the same thing (which, Heavenly Father supposedly came from a planet near the made-up star, "Kolob," once being a man like us), then there would have to be an infinite number

---

[303] *Doctrine and Covenants*, 93:33; If "man is *spirit*" (which is eternal) and the "elements are eternal," and "spirit and element are inseparably connected" then man is eternal. If man is eternal and Heavenly Father is physical, then physical bodies need to be in physical places. Therefore, physical places must be eternal.

of planets as well, at least accumulating at the speed of the number of people who die and have the chance to become gods of their own planets. If one were to think, *This is absurd!* By now, he would be correct. An actual, physical, infinite number of anything cannot exist.

In chapter two, I mentioned that in Mormonism, one must believe that there is a multiverse, *or* that the universe itself existed forever in order to believe that Mormonism is true. In other words, this is what Mormon theology requires to be logically consistent in such. The reason that an infinite universe, as opposed to a multiverse, was more likely in the mind of Smith is because the multiverse theory was not even in existence at the time of Joseph Smith. In either case, this requires there to be an endless number of gods, as well as an endless number of planets in our universe.

The point in all of this is that everything in the space-time continuum must have a beginning. The universe, in which all these planets exist in the mind of Joseph Smith, must have a beginning. Since there is a beginning, there cannot be an infinite amount of past time, based on the principle of causality.

Here again is the question we ask our Mormon friends: With all of these planets, or worlds, as the books describe, and the people becoming gods, who is it that made this law? Why do men become gods? If this has been happening from infinite regress, *which is literally impossible because we arrive at today*, then where did this law come from that says that men will become gods if they are good enough?

The problem here is that in Mormonism, there is no answer. In order for there to be an answer, there would have to be an ultimate beginning of the universe, someone to start it all, but this is not the case in Mormonism. All Heavenly Fathers in Mormonism have been exalted to Heavenly Father status by obeying "the Law of the gods" according to *Doctrine and Covenants*, in section one hundred and thirty-two, et al. At this point that we are discussing this because Mormons already believe in a "god" and therefore, we should be showing them how their belief in Heavenly Father is false, through this question of why is it that men can become "gods?"[304]

Fortunately, there is a real answer to this question: the answer is that Mormon doctrine is false. It is not only false logically, archaeologically, theologically, but also philosophically, as we have seen. Think of it like this: even if infinite regress was a thing, that still does not answer why this law is in effect. This law of men becoming gods literally transcends Mormonism! In a twisted, roundabout way, this argues that there is one God (as I have revealed in chapter four with the Mormon Cosmological Argument for One Supreme God), not many gods, as we would find in Mormon theology (monolatry/henotheism). One Supreme God would have to set this law in effect in order for men to become gods of their own worlds. The Supreme God would have to exist in order for any Heavenly Father to exist.

At this point, it is good to remind the reader that this is all really an easy concept to understand and even memorize. We all know that Mormons believe that they can become gods if they work hard enough at it. The problem is, *why is this the case*? Who wrote the Law of the gods if there is no single Supreme Being?

———————◆———————

There are innumerable claims of truth. The real concerns are about theology, reality, and life: where we come from, how we are supposed to live, and what happens when we die. Some claims deserve more attention than others. The truth claims that the *Doctrine and Covenants* makes about the reality of God screams for attention simply because, like all other religions, it claims exclusive knowledge about what happens when we die.

---

[304]The issue is that in Mormonism it is even possible to become a god.

"Then said Jesus to those Jews which believed on him, *'If ye continue in my word, then are ye my disciples indeed; And ye shall know the truth, and the truth shall make you free.'*" ~John 8:31–32.

Appendix

Memorable Questions to Ask Mormons

<u>**Who**</u> exactly are the Lamanites?

- DNA testing shows that the Native Americans (Lamanites) are not of Hebrew descent.

<u>**What**</u> is the cause of the doctrine of exaltation?

- 1. If the Law of the gods transcends these gods in Mormonism, then there is one Supreme God who wrote the Law or caused its existence.
  2. The Law of the gods transcends all Mormon gods (Heavenly Fathers).
  3. Therefore, there is one supreme God, who is the author of the law.

<u>**Where**</u> is the archaeological record?

- Why does the entire world not recognize the *Book of Mormon* as an accurate archaeological record, but archaeologists use the Bible to research locations, geography, and even relics? Stick to the subject. Don't let them jump around or change the subject.

When did Moroni become a god?

- Moroni became an angel, which does not make any sense because when a good person dies who knows the "restored gospel," he becomes a god, not an angel, as the *Doctrine and Covenants* clearly says.

Why is the *Book of Mormon* written in *King James Version* language when no one spoke like that at the time it was translated?

- Joseph Smith had presuppositions about such a language.

How is Jesus a created being if the Bible says that he is always the same and has always existed?

- See Hebrews 13:8 and John 1:1-3.

Sources Cited

Primary Sources:

Benson, Ezra Taft, Gordon B. Hinckley, and Thomas S. Monson. *First Presidency Statement on the King James Version of the Bible* Salt Lake City: The Church of Jesus Christ of the Latter-day Saints. August 1992. https://www.churchofjesuschrist.org/study/ensign/1992/08/news-of-the-church/first-presidency-statement-on-the-king-james-version-of-the-bible?lang=eng

The Church of Jesus Christ of the Latter-day Saints. *Church History Topics: Joseph Smith and Plural Marriage.* Salt Lake City: The Church of Jesus Christ of the Latter-day Saints. https://www.churchofjesuschrist.org/study/history/topics/joseph-smith-and-plural-marriage.

The Church of Jesus Christ of Latter-day Saints. *True to the Faith: A Gospel Reference.* Salt Lake City: The Church of Jesus Christ of the Latter-day Saints. Intellectual Reserve, Incorporated. 2004.

The Church of Jesus Christ of the Latter-day Saints. *Gospel Topics: Kingdoms of Glory.* The Church of Jesus Christ of the Latter-day Saints. https://www.churchofjesuschrist.org/study/manual/gospel-topics/kingdoms-of-glory?lang=eng.

The Church of Jesus Christ of Latter-day Saints. *Gospel Principles.* Salt Lake City. Intellectual Reserve, Incorporated, 2011: https://abn.churchofjesuschrist.org/study/manual/gospel-principles/chapter-47-Exaltation.

The Church of Jesus Christ of the Latter-day Saints. *Godhead.* The Church of Jesus Christ of the Latter-day Saints: Newsroom: https://newsroom. churchofjesuschrist.org/article/godhead

The Church of Jesus Christ of the Latter-day Saints. *Guide to the Scriptures.* Salt Lake City: The Church of Jesus Christ of the Latter-day Saints. Intellectual Reserve, Incorporated. 2013: https://www.churchofjesuschrist. org/study/scriptures/gs/introduction?lang=eng

The Church of Jesus Christ of the Latter-day Saints. *Gospel Topics Essays: Plural marriage in Kirtland and Nauvoo.* Salt Lake City: The Church of Jesus Christ of the Latter-day Saints: https:// www.churchofjesuschrist.org/study/manual/gospel-topics-essays/ plural-marriage-in-kirtland-and-nauvoo?lang=eng.

Faithful Answers Informed Response. *About.* FAIR: The Foundation for Apologetic Information and Research, 2022: https://www. fairlatterdaysaints.org/about

Faithful Answers Informed Response. *Question: Do Mormon men believe that they will become "Gods of their own planets" and rule over others?* FAIR: The Foundation for Apologetic Information and Research, 2022: https://www.fairlatterdaysaints.org/answers/Question:_Do_Mormon_ men_believe_that_they_will_become_%22gods_of_their_own_ planets%22_and_rule_over_others%3F

Gospel Media. *Do Latter-day Saints Believe in the Bible?* The Church of Jesus Christ of the Latter-day Saints. 2019: https://www.churchofjesuschrist. org/media/video/2019-07-0020-the-holy-bible-a-witness-of-jesus-christ.

Lund, Gerald N. *Is President Lorenzo Snow's oft-repeated statement—"As man now is, God once was; as God now is, man may be"—accepted as official doctrine by the Church?* Salt Lake City: The Church of Jesus Christ of the Latter-day Saints, 1982: https://abn.churchofjesuschrist.org/ study/ensign/1982/02/i-have-a-question/is-president-snows-statement- as-man-now-is-god-once-was-as-god-now-is-man-may-be-accepted-as- official-doctrine.html.

Ludlow, Daniel H. *Encyclopedia of Mormonism: the history, scripture, doctrine and procedure of the Church of Jesus Christ of the Latter-day Saints.* New York: Macmillan Publishing Company, 1992: Nauvoo Expositor; https://contentdm.lib.byu.edu/digital/collection/EoM/id/3984.

Smith, Joseph. *The Doctrine and Covenants of the Church of Jesus Christ of the Latter-day Saints.* Salt Lake City: The Church of Jesus Christ of the Latter-day Saints; Intellectual Reserve, 1981.

Smith, Joseph. *The Pearl of Great Price.* Salt Lake City: The Church of Jesus Christ of Latter-day Saints Intellectual Reserve, Inc., 1981.

Smith, Joseph. *The Book of Mormon: Another testament of Jesus Christ.* Salt Lake City: The Church of Jesus Christ of the Latter-day Saints: Intellectual Reserve, 1981.

Smith, Joseph. *History of The Church of Jesus Christ of Latter-day Saints, 7 volumes, edited by Brigham H. Roberts.* Salt Lake City: Deseret Book, 1957.

Smith, Joseph. *History of the Church of Jesus Christ of Latter-day Saints: The Articles of Faith, Volume 4.* Salt Lake City: Deseret Book, 1957.

Smith, Joseph. *Joseph Smith Translation.* Published by the Church of Jesus Christ of Latter-day Saints. Joseph Smith, I.L. Rogers, E. Robinson, publishing committee. 1867.

Smith, Joseph. *History of the Church of Jesus Christ of the Latter-day Saints.* Brigham Young University Studies, Deseret Book Company, 1948. https://byustudies.byu.edu/content/volume-4-chapter-27.

Smith, Joseph. *The Testimony of the Prophet Joseph Smith.* Salt Lake City: Church of Jesus Christ of the Latter-day Saints. 2013. https://www.churchofjesuschrist.org/study/scriptures/bofm/js?lang=ase.

Smith, Joseph. *Scriptural Teachings of the Prophet Joseph Smith.* Salt Lake City: Deseret Book Company, 1938: https://scriptures.byu.edu/stpjs.html

Snow, Lorenzo. *Teachings of the Presidents of the Church: Lorenzo Snow.* Utah: Church of Jesus Christ of the Latter-day

Saints. Intellectual Reserve, Incorporated. 2012: https://www.churchofjesuschrist.org/study/manual/teachings-of-presidents-of-the-church-lorenzo-snow/chapter-5-the-grand-destiny-of-the-faithful?lang=eng.

Turner, Rodney. *Prophecies and Promises of the Doctrine and Covenants.* The Church of Jesus Christ of the Latter-day Saints, 1972: https://abn.churchofjesuschrist.org/study/ensign/1972/12/prophecies-and-promises-of-the-doctrine-and-covenants.

Young, Brigham. *Journal of Discourses volume 4.* Liverpool: S. W. Richards, 1857. Public Domain: https://contentdm.lib.byu.edu/digital/collection/JournalOfDiscourses3/id/541.

Young, Brigham. *Teachings of Presidents of the Church.* Salt Lake City: The Church of Jesus Christ of Latter-day Saints, 1997: https://www.churchofjesuschrist.org/study/manual/teachings-brigham-young/chapter-13?lang=eng.

Secondary Sources:

Aland, Kurt, et al. *The Greek New Testament, Fourth Revised Edition (with Morphology)* Deutsche Bibelgesellschaft, 1993; 2006.

Beckwith, Francis and Stephen Parrish, *See the Gods Fall: Four rivals to Christianity* Joplin: College Press Publishing Company, 1997.

Blomberg, Craig *The Historical Reliability of the New Testament.* Nashville: B&H Academic, 2016.

Corduan, Winfried. *Neighboring Faiths: A Christian introduction to world religions.* Downers Grove: InterVarsity Press, 2012.

Craig, William Lane. *Doctrine of the Trinity (part 1).* Reasonable Faith, June 27, 2011: https://www.reasonablefaith.org/podcasts/defenders-podcast-series-2/s2-doctrine-of-god-trinity/doctrine-of-the-trinity-part-1.

Craig, William Lane. *On Guard: Defending your faith with reason and precision*. Colorado Springs: David C. Cook, 2010.

Craig, William Lane. *Reasonable Faith: Christian truth and apologetics*. Wheaton: Crossway, 2008.

Carson, D. A. Ed. *Telling the Truth: Evangelizing Postmoderns*. Grand Rapids: Zondervan, 2000.

Damer, T. Edward. *Attacking Faulty Reasoning: A practical guide to fallacy-free arguments 7th edition*. Boston: Wadsworth, 2013.

Dawkins, Richard. *The Selfish Gene, 2nd ed*. Oxford: Oxford University Press 1989.

The Department of Anthropology Smithsonian Institution. *Inquiry concerning the Smithsonian Institution's alleged use of the Book of Mormon as a scientific guide*. National Museum of Natural History Smithsonian Institution., 1996. https://www.mrm.org/smithsonian

Easton, M.G. *Easton's Bible Dictionary*. Oak Harbor, WA: Logos Research Systems, Inc., 1996, c1897.

Eklund, Matthew. *The Mormon Chameleon: The Ever-changing Gospel of the LDS Church (Part One)*. Beggars Bread July 2020: https://beggarsbread.org/2020/07/19/the-mormon-chameleon-the-ever-changing-gospel-of-the-lds-church-part-one/.

Frances, Allen J. M.D. *Multiple Personality: Mental Disorder, Myth, or Metaphor? Why multiple personality disorder fads come and go*. Psychology Today, Jan 30, 2014: https://www.psychologytoday.com/us/blog/saving-normal/201401/multiple-personality-mental-disorder-myth-or-metaphor.

Ford, Governor Thomas. *History of Illinois from its commencement as a state in 1818 TO 1847* Chicago: SC GRIGGS & CO 1854: http://livinghistoryofillinois.com/pdf_files/History%20of%20Illinois%20from%20it%27s%20Commencement%20as%20a%20State%20in%201814%20to%201847.pdf

Garland, David E. *1 Corinthians: Baker Exegetical Commentary on the New Testament*. Baker Academic: Grand Rapids, 2003.

Geisler, Norman L. and Ronald M. Brooks. *When Skeptics Ask: A handbook on Christian evidences*. Grand Rapids: Baker Books, 2013.

Geisler, Norman and Ron Rhodes, *Conviction Without Compromise*. Eugene: Harvest House Publishers, 2008.

Geisler, Norman and Joseph M. Holden. *The Popular Handbook of Archaeology and the Bible*. Eugene: Harvest House Publishers, 2013, 122;

Geisler, Norman and William L. Nix. *From God to us: How we got our Bible*. Chicago: Moody Publishers, 2012.

Geisler, Norman and Frank Turek. *I Don't Have Enough Faith to Be an Atheist*. Wheaton: Crossway, 2004.

Geisler, Norman L. and Ronald M. Brooks. *Come, Let Us Reason: An introduction to logical thinking*. Grand Rapids, 1990.

Geisler, Norman. *Systematic Theology*. Bloomington: Bethany House Publishers, 2011.

Geisler, Norman and David Geisler. *Conversational Evangelism*. Eugene: Harvest House Publishers, 2009.

Holden, Joseph and Norman Geisler, *The Popular Handbook of Archaeology*. Eugene: Harvest House Publishers, 2013.

Jefferson, Thomas. *Thomas Jefferson's Bible*. Smithsonian National Museum of American History. Kenneth E. Behring Center. Date unknown. https://americanhistory.si.edu/JeffersonBible/the-book/

Jewish Virtual Library. *Archaeology in Israel: Qumran*. American-Israeli Cooperative Enterprise, 2022: https://www.jewishvirtuallibrary.org/qumran.

Johnson, Eric and Sean McDowell. *Sharing the Good News with Mormons*. Eugene: Harvest House Publishers, 2018.

Janosik, Daniel. *The Guide to Answering Islam: What every Christian needs to know about Islam and the rise of radical Islam.* Cambridge: Christian Publishing House, 2019.

Josephus, Flavius and William Whiston, *The Works of Josephus: Complete and Unabridged.* Peabody: Hendrickson, 1996, c1987.

Lewis, Clive. *Mere Christianity.* New York: HarperCollins Publishers, 1996.

Hone, William. *The Lost Books of the Bible: The Gospel According to Peter.* New York: Gramercy Books, 1979.

Martin, Walter. *The Kingdom of the Cults.* Bloomington: Bethany House, 2003.

Muncaster, Ralph. *Can Archaeology Prove the New Testament?* Eugene: Harvest House Publishers, 2000.

Merriam-Webster, Merriam-Webster's Collegiate Dictionary. Springfield, MA: Merriam-Webster, Incorporated, 2003.

Mounce, William D. *What I Have learned About Greek and Translation: Since Joining the CBT.* Grand Rapids: Zondervan, 2017.

Pollard, Nick. *Evangelism Made Slightly Less Difficult: how to interest people who aren't interested.* Downers Grove: InterVarsity Press, 1997.

Roberts, Alexander, James Donaldson, and A. Cleveland Coxe, eds., *"The Encyclical Epistle of the Church at Smyrna," in The Apostolic Fathers with Justin Martyr and Irenaeus, vol. 1, The Ante-Nicene Fathers* Buffalo, NY: Christian Literature Company, 1885.

Shakir, M. H. ed. *The Quran.* Medford, MA: Perseus Digital Library, n.d.

Shanks, Hershel and Ben Witherington III. *The Brother of Jesus: The dramatic story & meaning of the first archaeological link to Jesus & His family.* New York: HarperCollins Publishers, 2003.

Strong, Augustus Hopkins. *Systematic Theology.* Bellingham: Logos Research Systems, Inc., 2004.

Schaff, Philip and David Schley Schaff. *History of the Christian Church.* Oak Harbor, WA: Logos Research Systems, Inc., 1997.

Wallace, J. Warner. *Cold-Case Christianity: A homicide detective investigates the claims of the gospels*. Colorado Springs: David C. Cook, 2013.

Wilder, Lynn. *Unveiling Grace: The story of how we found our way out of the Mormon Church* Grand Rapids: Zondervan, 2013.

Index

Alexamenos Graffito, 124-125

Apologetics, 2-8, 150-179

Archaeology, 118-129

As far as it is translated correctly, 28-29

As we are now, 13, 27, 33-34, 45, 57, 59, 95, 100, 162

Atheism, 38, 155-156

Beyond reasonable doubt, 127, 142

Buddhism, 30

Celestial Kingdom, 51-54

Christianese, 163

Cosmological metaphysics, 23, 105

Criminal motivation, 90

Dead Sea Scrolls, 119

Definitions, 54, 148, 161

Deism, 155

Demon, 71-74, 90-91

Early Modern English, 64

Eternal, 14, 35, 54-61

Eternal progression, 22, 48, 53-54, 61

Exclusivity, 138-141, 178

FAIR, 38-41

Fundamental laws of logic, 22, 56, 61, 79-80, 102, 140, 148, 142, 159-160,

Generations, 23, 35, 98, 102

Genetic fallacy, 128

Gospel barriers, 157-159

Heavenly Mother, 21, 23, 34, 66, 89

Henotheism/monolatry, 17-18, 156, 178

Hinduism, 30, 139-141

Infinite regress, xi, 22, 35, 106, 147, 161, 176-178

Islam, 5n13, 26n41, 66, 71-89, 152n267, 168

James Ossuary, 126-127

Joseph Smith Translation, 135-138, 153

Kalam Cosmological Argument, 98, 102, 161

Karma, 30, 106

Koine Greek, 73, 86, 103, 135, 153

Kolob, 34, 52, 147, 176

Law of the gods, 29-31, 33, 37-38, 41, 44, 69, 95-96, 100-106, 111n175, 117, 129, 149, 161, 165, 177-178, 181

Like god, 40, 97, 177

Lord of the Rings, 87

Lorenzo Snow Couplet, xn3, 7-8, 19, 22, 46-47, 97, 100, 147, 175-176

Manuscripts, 86, 133-136, 144, 162

Martyrdom of Polycarp, 65

Megiddo Mosaic Inscription, 123-124

Metaphysics, 23, 105

Modernity, 151

Monarchotheism, 17-18

Mormon Cosmological Argument for the Existence of One Supreme God, 105, 117, 159-161, 178

Moroni Challenge, 5-7, 45, 151-152, 164

Nauvoo Expositor, 68-71, 129

New Jerusalem, 82-83

Oak tree, 31

Omniscience, 56-59

Panentheism, 156

Pantheism, 156

Physical infinites, 22, 35-37, 49-50, 55, 63, 96-100, 104-106, 147-149, 161, 176-178

Poisoning the well, 139

Polygamy, 69, 74-75

Polytheism, 17-18, 139, 155

Pontius Pilate Inscription, 122-123

Postmodernism, 7, 44-45, 150-155

Powerful, 61, 109-110

Pragmatism, 136

Presuppositions, 64, 91, 153-156

Priesthood, 14, 53, 55, 90, 134

Principle of causality, 30, 95, 98-105, 160-161, 177

Prophet, seer, and revelator, 16-17, 47

Psychology, 113

Questions, 5-8, 43-50, 181-182

Red herring, xn5, 33, 46, 49

Restored gospel, 131-139, 182

Risks, 168-170

Satan, 2-3, 71-73, 100, 115, 148, 162

Second Law of Thermodynamics, 99

Self-control, 66, 90

Sex, 64-76, 88-90

Shema, 12, 111, 114

Sin Janitor, 79, 166

Six-barreled pistol, 65

Smithsonian Institute, 120-121

Soteriology, 26, 96, 138

Supreme Being, 18, 48, 54-61, 96, 101-102, 106, 117

Taqiyya, 5, 45, 47

The Great Blacksmith, 105-106

The Ten Commandments, 101, 171

Theism, 155, 158

Tithe, 90-91

Transcend, 37, 52, 96, 101, 103-105, 117, 146, 159, 161, 178, 181

Tritheism, 12, 110, 117

Trilemma, 64, 67, 147

Trinitarian, 11-13, 110-117, 137

Trinity, see "Trinitarian"

Truth, x-xi, 1-10, 22-23, 27n44, 39, 43, 45, 64, 95, 100, 144-148, 150-160

Worlds/planets, 20, 30, 36-37, 49-50, 97, 175, 177

Printed in the USA
CPSIA information can be obtained
at www.ICGtesting.com
CBHW052134091023
1283CB00004B/43

.